200 EASY SLOW COOKER RECIPES

KATIE BISHOP

HarperCollins*Publishers*
77-85 Fulham Palace Road,
Hammersmith, London W6 8JB

www.harpercollins.co.uk

1 2 3 4 5 6 7 8 9 10

All the recipes in this book have been previously published in *Slow Cooking* and
More Slow Cooker Recipes.

Text © Katie Bishop (2008, 2009)
Photographs © Steve Baxter (2013, 2009) apart from the following which are
© David Munns (2008): pages 31, 32, 40, 45, 56, 59, 67, 118, 139, 149, 185, 219,
238, 245, 253 and 257.

Slow cookers were kindly loaned by Lakeland Limited. www.lakeland.co.uk

Katie Bishop asserts her moral right to be identified as the author of this work.

A catalogue record of this book is available from the British Library.

ISBN 978-0-00-749869-7

Printed and bound in China by RR Donnelly

CONTENTS

INTRODUCTION

This book is designed to be really simple to use. If you fancy a curry or something spicy then look in the curries section, or maybe rich braises and stews are the reason you have a slow cooker in your kitchen, so take a look at that chapter. In my kitchen my slow cookers (cookers are plural because at the last count I had eight!) are a godsend for midweek meals, but particularly when entertaining.

This book is intended to complement a busy lifestyle, providing ideas for slow-cooked food for busy people. All the recipes have been written with the time-conscious in mind, for those who like good-quality (and that doesn't mean expensive!), great tasting food, but may not necessarily have hours in which to prepare it. There are also recipes for those with the inclination to do a little more advance preparation, and those who would rather throw it all into a pot and forget about it! Either way, as working late and/or lengthy socialising become the norm, you can feel confident that slow-cooked food can, in the majority of cases, be left happily for longer than the designated cooking time without spoiling, overcooking or burning.

The 200 unbelievably tasty, gorgeous and sumptuous dishes within this book will, I hope, convince you that over a long period of time some ingredients evolve into something even more spectacular than would be achieved with conventional cooking, often with significantly less time-consuming attention and hassle.

I love to have large gatherings and parties, and it is at these times I could not live without a slow cooker. Entertaining for a large number has never been easier, so if that's your thing, you'll also find a chapter for special occasions and celebrations. There are also yummy chapters on roasts, light and easy dishes, chillies and pasta sauces as well as puddings and cakes. So, whatever your penchant and requirements, whether after-work suppers or make-ahead meals for those days when you just don't want to spend too much time in the kitchen, there should be a chapter for you!

Either way, I hope you enjoy the recipes. They have all been lovingly and very thoroughly tested. As mentioned earlier, do continue to bear in mind that every slow cooker is different and yours may be a different size from that used in this book, so times will vary accordingly. I'm sure you'll soon get to know and love your machine and be able to adapt all the recipes with ease. Treat your slow cooker well and it will be a faithful companion for many years to come!

Katie

Rolled shoulder of lamb with cumin and harissa (see page 168)

THE EASY GUIDE TO SLOW COOKING

If you haven't used a slow cooker before then this section is definitely worth reading. Indeed, if you've been using a slow cooker for a while and are starting to feel a bit bored with the results, then some of these guidelines may just remind you of the many possibilities of your slow cooker and help you expand your repertoire.

WHY TRY SLOW COOKING?

It's affordable and economical Slow cooking turns undervalued and underused cuts like shins, hocks, necks and brisket into beautiful tender pieces of meat. These cuts are much more affordable than the ever-popular cuts like rump, fillet and sirloin, and have the added value of using up parts of the carcass that may otherwise have been forgotten. Using as much of the animal as possible is good for your wallet, respectful to the animal and critical to farmers' livelihoods.

It's energy efficient Slow cookers are also very energy efficient; again allowing you to save money, plus they cook in an environmentally responsible way. Some slow-cooking methods can save up to five times the energy of stove-top cooking since heat is retained rather than being lost to the air, and that has to be a good thing for the planet. Most slow cookers use as little energy as a domestic light bulb. From a practical point of view this also makes cooking more pleasant as the kitchen doesn't steam up and get as hot as it would during conventional cooking.

It's delicious! Slow-cooked foods are often redolent of the winter months when stews, casseroles and soups are popular, but the advantage of a cooler kitchen makes slow cooking in the summer just as appealing. Slow cooking suits the needs of many of us who have little time; it reflects popular trends in the restaurant industry, as well as supporting farmers and making a small contribution to the environment. But, most importantly, slow-cooked food tastes great! Long, gentle cooking allows food to develop flavour in a different way to rapid cooking. It coaxes out flavours that are slower to develop and encourages the flavours of individual ingredients to marry together and blend in a unique way.

HOW SAFE IS SLOW COOKING?

One of the questions I am asked most about slow cooking is, 'Is it safe?' Concerns can range from food safety to worries about fire and energy consumption.

Will slow cooking heat my food safely? A slow cooker will operate at about 77–97°C (171–207°F), depending on its selected temperature setting and manufacturer's variations. In England a temperature of 75°C (167°F) is deemed adequate to destroy any harmful bacteria. Once food has reached this temperature, it can be kept at a lower temperature for up to 2 hours and still be consumed safely. So, a slow cooker that has been given time to warm up and reach its optimum temperature at the designated setting will safely destroy the risk of food poisoning. If you are in any doubt, I suggest you stick to cooking pieces of meat, as opposed to whole birds or joints and/or invest in a simple cooking thermometer for inserting into ingredients to test their core temperature.

If I still have to convince you of the safety of your machine, then you can also turn the slow cooker onto high for the first hour of cooking to bring the temperature to above 75°C (167°F). However, I rarely do this, and remain alive to tell the tale! My view is that if you begin with fresh ingredients, use clean utensils and a clean thermometer, there is no reason why you should have any concerns at all about food safety with your slow cooker.

Can I use my slow cooker to reheat food? Food should never be reheated in a slow cooker (although Christmas pudding is safe), as it will not heat to a point where the food becomes safe from harmful bacteria and potential food poisoning bugs. Always reheat slow-cooked foods in a pan on the hob, in the microwave or in the oven. Equally, don't leave food to cool down in the slow cooker, as this will create the perfect conditions for unpleasant bugs to multiply – instead, always remove it to another dish.

Is it safe to leave my slow cooker unattended?
While talking about safety it's also important to point out that a slow cooker can be left on for many hours, unattended, but make sure you always follow the manufacturer's instructions for exact environmental safety precautions. With basic care, using a slow cooker couldn't be simpler. In essence, all you need do is to fill the dish up with ingredients, put the lid on and set it to low or high to begin cooking.

Where should I put my slow cooker when in use? Despite being very economical and transferring a limited amount of heat and energy into the atmosphere, the area immediately around the slow cooker will become hot. So using your antique dining table as a base will not serve you well, potentially causing damage to the surface. Instead use a heatproof surface or worktop.

Do I always need to add liquid to my slow cooker? Check your manufacturer's instructions, but most slow cookers require at least some liquid in the base of the dish to operate properly. You may spot a couple of recipes in this book where this does not happen – this is because these recipes include ingredients that naturally contain a high level of moisture, or there is a large quantity of ingredients, which will create a lot of additional condensation quickly, and therefore a lot of moisture of their own. In some cases, using this method enables some caramelisation of the ingredients in the slow cooker with great results.

WHICH SLOW COOKER SHOULD YOU BUY?
There are a surprisingly large number of slow cookers available, which vary in size, shape, capacity and price. Prices are surprisingly low in the majority of cases, although as with most things, there is a product to appeal to every consumer and every pocket. As with any kitchen appliance or oven, each brand varies in terms of its heating speed and how evenly it cooks and, as with any oven or appliance, there is an element of getting used to your own model.

The important thing to remember is that every machine will be different. They will reach different top temperatures and be suited to different lengths of cooking and techniques. It is essential that you check the manufacturer's instructions for your machine before embarking on any of these recipes or any of your own creations.

What functions should I look out for in a slow cooker? Slow cookers are basically made up of a heated, electric element, which surrounds an inner dish with a lid. The cooker is plugged into the mains and controlled simply to high or low. You will also find options for timers, beepers, lights, digital screens... the list goes on, but for me there are two main factors when choosing a machine:
- **What size is it?**
- **And does it have a removable, ovenproof inner dish?**

Spicy seafood chowder (see page 38)

What size slow cooker will I need? Most slow cooker ranges will come in a choice of sizes. The capacity of your model will depend on the number of people you wish to cook for, and the type of food you want to cook. As a benchmark, a 5–6 litre (9–10½ pint) cooker should easily cater for six people. If you like to cook large batches of food for freezing, or entertaining, then a 6 litre (10½ pint) capacity model or more would be perfect for you. If you would like to cook joints of meat or larger cuts, then try an oval- shaped cooker. Round models tend to be better suited to soups, stews and puddings.

All the recipes in this book have been cooked and tested in a 5.7 litre (10 pint) slow cooker. If your slow cooker is a different size then you will need to adjust the ingredients and cooking times accordingly. If you find that recipes requiring tins or dishes to be placed inside the slow cooker are difficult to follow (because of the size of your slow cooker), then try using individual ramekins or ovenproof dishes instead, and adjust the cooking times accordingly. Please remember that every brand of slow cooker is different, so it's critical to follow the individual manufacturer's instructions.

Removable or fixed inner dish? Most major brands have a removable inner dish, although some fixed models are available. For flexibility, the removable models are far superior, especially ones that can be used on the hob to sauté – they create less washing up if meat and foods are seared before cooking, and most importantly they retain all the flavours and caramelised loveliness created by sautéing and searing.

Oven or grill suitable? Try to buy a model that's suitable for heating in the oven or under a grill – this will give you increased options in terms of finishing dishes to give them colour after cooking.

Digital timer? A machine with an in-built digital timer is also a real advantage in terms of ease and convenience and is definitely worth paying a little extra for.

HOW MUCH PREPARATION DO I NEED?

In many cases your preparation will change according to how and when you are cooking your food. If, for example, you are starting your cooking in the morning so that it cooks while you are at work, ready for your return home, then throwing everything into the slow cooker in the quickest possible time will be essential. In this book there are lots of simple ideas that can be thrown together quickly and then left to their own devices.

Likewise, making a recipe that will cook overnight will require preparation just before you go to bed. So recipes in this instance are short and sweet in the main, with the odd exception for night owls or those with insomnia!

If you are cooking for a large number of people, making sauces, chutneys and jams, or baking cakes and desserts, then allow slightly more time for preparation prior to cooking, but none of the recipes in this book will extend beyond 30 minutes of preparation time.

Turkey ballotine with chestnuts and port (see page 152)

Importantly, the slow cooker is versatile enough to make all of these types of cooking possible and give good, reliable and above all consistent results every time.

HOW TO COOK WITH YOUR SLOW COOKER
Slow-cooked food should be left to its own devices, so unless the recipe suggests it, food is best left un-stirred with the lid sealed and undisturbed. As tempting as it may seem, lifting the lid to check on progress will cause the cooker to lose heat and moisture, which can affect the quality of the final dish. This is particularly important in the first hour or so of cooking, as this is the time that the cooker is heating the food to a safe and optimal temperature.

It's also worth acknowledging that a slow cooker is completely different from a pressure cooker and will have very different results – they are not comparable, although there seems to be a popular belief that they are one and the same thing.

How should I layer and fill my slow cooker? It's easy to get carried away and overfill your slow cooker – aim to fill the inner dish about half full, or ideally no more than two-thirds full, and certainly no more than 4cm (1½in) from the top. Place the ingredients that take the longest time to cook, such as root vegetables and large cuts of meat, on the bottom of the slow cooker dish so they have maximum heat exposure. Less hardy ingredients, such as rice, pasta, dairy products and certain more delicate vegetables, should be added at the end of cooking, usually during the last hour or so. Resist the temptation to lift the lid of the slow cooker or stir the contents, as doing so will affect the temperature in the cooker and allow all-important moisture to escape during cooking. However, if you find that your slow cooker has 'hot spots', then you may find occasional stirring helpful to encourage even cooking.

When should I add seasoning? Slow cooking affects the flavour of food in a different way to conventional methods. As a result it is a good idea to season your food at the end of cooking, unless otherwise stated in the recipe (a common exception would be when cooking certain vegetables, when seasoning can help to concentrate their flavour). When cooking with brown rice, beans or pulses, I always season at the end of cooking, whether slow or conventional, as the salt can toughen the outer husk, making it chewy and less pleasant to eat. It's also a good idea to add soft herbs, such as parsley, basil and mint, towards the end of cooking to avoid their discoloration and loss of flavour.

Can I freeze my slow cooked dishes? The flavour of any stew, curry or casserole is undoubtedly enhanced if it is left to cool, chilled overnight and reheated the next day (this also allows you to remove some of the fat that will have solidified on the surface). In addition, these foods also tend to freeze brilliantly. If you, like me, are a fan of freezing, then there are a few things to consider. Ideally, transfer any leftovers out of the slow cooker to allow them to cool – this will be preferable to cooling them in the already warm slow cooker, which could encourage the growth of bacteria. Store leftovers in shallow, covered containers and refrigerate or freeze within 2 hours of cooking.

Can I defrost and reheat slow cooker food? Defrost any frozen foods thoroughly in the fridge before reheating. Never reheat food in your slow cooker as it will not reach a safe temperature for long enough. Cooked foods should be reheated on the hob, in a microwave or in a conventional oven until piping hot. The hot food can then be placed in a preheated slow cooker to keep it hot for serving, if you wish. Never use frozen ingredients in your slow cooker. The heat in your slow cooker is likely to be unevenly distributed, which could result in some ingredients not reaching a safe and hygienic temperature. It would also create a lot of excess liquid, which a slow cooker is ill-equipped to get rid of. The ceramic insert in a slow cooker can crack if exposed to sudden temperature changes, so it's a good idea not to put a ceramic slow cooker dish into a preheated base straight from the fridge. Equally avoid putting a hot slow cooker dish directly onto a cold surface, even if that surface is heatproof.

Do I need to brown meat and vegetables before adding to the slow cooker? Your slow cooker will cope admirably if you throw some ingredients in and leave it to its own devices. However, when cooking with meat and vegetables, and if you have plenty of time, you might like to brown them first. This will give the dish extra colour as well as flavour. In addition, it will render fattier cuts of meat, removing some excess fat, which is healthier for us and can also result in a better dish. In my recipes, however, I am always conscious of saving time, so I only include browning if it makes a significant difference to the finished dish.

How should I treat fatty meat in the slow cooker? For more even cooking, trim excess fat from meats, as high-fat foods cook more quickly than other ingredients, such as vegetables. If you're making a recipe with both meat and root vegetables, it is often a good idea to make a bed of vegetables on the bottom of the dish and place the meat on top, so that it cooks evenly. Saying that, foods high in fat aren't necessarily a bad thing for slow cooking. This 'good' fat comes from intramuscular fat running through certain cuts of meat, as opposed to the layer of fat on the surface of meat.

How much liquid should I use? Slow cooking does not allow for the evaporation that occurs in other cooking methods, so it is advisable to reduce the amount of liquid you would usually use in conventional recipes. You can usually do this by up to 50 per cent, although as a general rule of thumb I use about one-third less liquid than in my conventional recipes. If you want a thicker, less watery sauce try removing the lid and increasing the setting to high to allow for some of the excess to evaporate. Alternatively, transfer the

sauce to a saucepan and boil over a high heat for a much faster reduction method. You could also sprinkle a little plain flour over the ingredients in the slow cooker dish before cooking to achieve a thicker sauce.

Can I bake with my slow cooker? Baking in a slow cooker defies many regular rules, but it is possible. I either grease and line the slow cooker dish thoroughly with butter and baking parchment or use an ovenproof dish or dishes and use the slow cooker as a water bath (also called a bain marie). Both methods work well and are suited to light cakes and sponges, and especially custards and similar dishes.

Your manufacturer's instructions will also give you a further indication of your machine's suitability for baking. In most cases you will need to preheat the slow cooker and may need to cook on high if you are using raising agents. Check individual recipes for specific guidelines.

Temperatures and timings Personal preference and differences in slow cooker models will always create variations in cooking times and temperatures. However, most recipes can be adapted for slow cooking. Simply follow the guidelines above and cook until tender. As a basic rule of thumb, a recipe that cooks for 1½–2 hours on the hob will probably take about 4 hours on high in the slow cooker. This would translate to 8 hours on the low setting. I generally prefer cooking on the low setting (unless baking, when I need a higher temperature to make things rise), as I feel the longer time period coaxes out even more flavour from the ingredients. It also ensures more even, thorough cooking.

Can I use a conventional recipe with a slow cooker? Most recipes are adaptable to slow cooking and this book gives a good indication of the different cooking methods that work particularly well, in what proportions and for how long. Areas of difficulty are baking, which is a very precise science and requires, in most cases, a blast of heat to encourage rising or to form a crust.

Desserts, fish, pasta and rice can all be cooked in the slow cooker but will start to denature during very long, all-day cooking, so that is best avoided for these ingredients. Some slow cookers can be used in the oven or under the grill and some (although still relatively few) can be used on a hob. Every slow cooker is different and individual manufacturer's instructions should be followed in each case. The slow cooker dish must always be removed from the outer casing before being put in the oven or under the grill. In most instances the removable dish will be ceramic or earthenware and is breakable if dropped and will chip if given reason to do so. The slow cooker base should never be cooked in, or immersed in water for cleaning, but simply wiped clean with a damp cloth.

Above all, this book is intended to be a fresh look at slow cooking, a book for how we live today. It offers some classic dishes and others that you probably never have considered possible in a slow cooker.

WHAT TYPE OF INGREDIENTS SHOULD YOU USE?
You can cook almost anything in a slow cooker, but for the best results choose the right ingredients.

When it comes to **meat**, even the most coarse cuts of meat can be transformed into meltingly soft, flavoursome delights! All you need is time and a few additional ingredients and the magic of slow cooking will do the rest. To get the most from any cut of meat it must be 'fit for purpose' or cooked appropriately. Lean, fine-grained cuts respond well to fast, high-temperature cooking, while tougher cuts with more connective tissue need long, slow cooking to make them tender. For me, knowing how to use and get the best from a whole carcass is something that every carnivorous cook should know about. You'll get the best, most varied eating experience, but vitally it makes the best economic sense – for cooks, butchers and farmers alike. Generally the slow cook cuts come from the parts of the animal that have to work the hardest – the forequarter

(neck, belly, shoulders) and the legs. These tough, sinewy muscles will taste dreadful if they are not cooked correctly, but so too would the finest fillet of beef. Using a moist method of cooking, or cooking these cuts in some well-seasoned liquid – whether it is stock, wine or even water – will work wonders. The liquid will encourage the muscles to relax their tough structure, and the gelatine that this process produces will, in turn, flavour the liquid to make wonderful gravy. Not only do these cuts present tremendous value for money, but they also taste great. It is also worth considering that cuts labelled 'stewing' will usually take longer to tenderise than those labelled 'braising'.

Fruit and vegetables vary too, some being rather more resilient to long slow cooking than others, despite the more delicate temperatures of the slow cooker. As you would expect, root vegetables will take longer cooking than soft, delicate vegetables like cauliflower and broccoli,

Gooey chocolate pudding (see page 264)

although you may be pleasantly surprised by vegetables cooked with their skins on, such as aubergines and courgettes, which one may otherwise expect to disintegrate with lengthy cooking. Unless otherwise stated, place vegetables in the slow cooker dish first then top with the meat, if using, as this will ensure that the vegetables cook evenly and absorb all the tasty meaty juices. Fruit follows a similarly logical path, soft fruit breaking down significantly faster than stone fruit or apples and pears, for example, and fruit in skins holding up remarkably well.

Cut **potatoes** will turn black (oxidise) when in contact with the air, as will cut apples, pears and bananas. These must either be completely immersed in liquid during cooking or coated in lemon juice to prevent this 'oxidisation' from happening.

Dairy products such as milk, cheese, cream and yoghurt and sugar tend to break down in the slow cooker after prolonged cooking (over 6 hours), especially when they are in concentrated form in cakes and desserts. However, a few hours are fine, and if well diluted, in water, for example, there are few issues. If in doubt, stir dairy products in at the end of cooking to finish a dish, rather than cook with them for the duration.

Pasta can be cooked in the slow cooker but will become unpleasantly soft if cooked for too long. Try adding pasta to slow-cooked sauces about 30 minutes before the end of cooking. Lasagne and cannelloni are, however, more successful in the slow cooker (see Red Pepper, Basil and Ricotta Cannelloni on page 54).

Rice will absorb lots of excess moisture produced during slow cooking and therefore lots of flavour too. Add about 30–50 minutes before the end of cooking and stir a couple of times to ensure that it cooks evenly. Baked risotto dishes also work very well (see the Pasta, Rice and Grains chapter for some great ideas).

Dried beans still need to be soaked overnight before slow cooking. Dried red kidney beans must also be boiled for at least 10 minutes and drained before cooking to remove their dangerous toxins. Other pulses – such as lentils, split peas and tinned beans – can be used directly, but will break up with a very extended period of cooking.

Frozen ingredients must be defrosted before use in the slow cooker, otherwise they are unlikely to reach a safe cooking temperature, making them food poisoning time bombs!

The cooking liquid is an important part of success in slow cooking. As water is not lost in slow cooking in the way it is during extended stove-top simmering, the amount of water used to cook foods is normally reduced by about one-third. Evaporation is reduced in the slow cooker as all the steam is retained in the pot; however, there is still some evaporation as the moisture/steam hits the hot sides of the cooking dish – this again will vary from one machine to another so keep an eye out when you are getting to know your cooker. Use water, stocks, wine, beer, cider, fruit juice or similar to cook in and add flavour. Bear in mind that when cooking with wine or vinegar the lack of evaporation means that the acidity and alcohol doesn't cook off in the same way as stove-top cooking, so the flavour usually remains very pungent and undeveloped.

While cooking in liquid is particularly useful in slow cooking, so too is the ability to use the slow cooker as a water bath (also called a bain-marie). Gone are the hours of checking and worrying about steamers and pans boiling dry – this simply doesn't happen in the slow cooker. A water bath is particularly useful when baking, creating a fantastically light sponge or creamy custard. It's good too in terms of cooking for long periods of time (clearly a moot point when discussing slow cooking, but in this instance a long period of time is 8–9 hours or perhaps overnight). It provides a very gentle cook so that whether cooking overnight or cooking something very delicate like a custard, the water bath produces a great result.

SOUPS, SALADS
+
LIGHT MEALS

VEGETABLE FRITTATA

Preparation time: 10 minutes
Cooking time: 2½–3 hours
Serves 6

3 peppers (preferably mixed colours), deseeded and cut into chunks

1 medium courgette, trimmed and cut into chunks

1 medium aubergine, trimmed and cut into chunks

1 red onion, peeled and cut into chunks

12 cherry tomatoes

2 garlic cloves, peeled and roughly chopped

12 new potatoes, washed and cut into quarters

3 fresh thyme sprigs

2 tbsp olive oil

Sea salt and freshly ground black pepper

8 eggs

10 tbsp grated Parmesan cheese

A simple fresh vegetable frittata looks wonderfully colourful and is a great way to use up seasonal vegetables in the summer months.

Place the peppers, courgette, aubergine and onion in the slow cooker dish and scatter the cherry tomatoes, garlic, new potatoes and thyme over the top.

Drizzle with the olive oil and season generously with salt and pepper. Mix well with a wooden spoon until all the vegetables are coated in the oil. Cover with the lid and cook on high, stirring occasionally, for 1½–2 hours or until tender. Remove the thyme and discard.

Whisk the eggs and half of the Parmesan cheese together in a bowl. Season generously, then pour the mixture over the vegetables. Replace the lid and cook for a further hour or until just set.

Remove from the slow cooker base and sprinkle with the remaining Parmesan cheese. Run a knife around the edge of the frittata to loosen, then leave to cool, uncovered, for 5 minutes before cutting into wedges or squares to serve.

AUBERGINE AND CARDAMOM BABA GANOUSH

Baba ganoush is great as a dip with crudités or as part of a more substantial meal with mezze and pitta bread. In this version, cardamom gives the aubergine a sweet and fragrant flavour.

Remove the green outer husks of the cardamom pods leaving only the black seeds behind and crush these lightly in a mortar with a pestle.

In a large bowl, mix the olive oil and lemon juice together, then add the crushed cardamom seeds and garlic. Season with salt and pepper and mix well. Add the aubergine halves and toss in the dressing until evenly coated, then place them in the slow cooker dish. Cover with the lid and cook on high for 2½ hours.

Remove the aubergines from the slow cooker dish and leave to cool slightly. When cool enough to handle, scoop the aubergine flesh out of the skins with a spoon and place in a large bowl. Add the yogurt and mix well. Season to taste.

Spoon the mixture into a serving dish and drizzle more olive oil generously over the top. Serve with warm pitta bread and salad as an appetiser or light lunch.

COOKING CONVENTIONALLY?
Place the aubergines in a baking dish, cover with foil and cook in an oven preheated to 180°C (350°F), Gas mark 4 for 1–2 hours until tender, then continue as above.

Preparation time: 15 minutes
Cooking time: 2½ hours
Serves 2–3 as a main course
Vegetarian

20 cardamom pods

2 tbsp extra virgin olive oil, plus extra for drizzling

1 tbsp lemon juice

1 garlic clove, peeled and crushed

Sea salt and freshly ground black pepper

2 medium aubergines, about 250g (9oz) each, cut in half lengthways

2 tbsp Greek yogurt

MOROCCAN FILLED PEPPERS

Preparation time: 10 minutes
Cooking time: 1½-2 hours
Serves **4**
Vegetarian

4 red peppers

2 garlic cloves, peeled and finely sliced

6 tbsp couscous

3 tbsp boiling water

4 tbsp finely chopped fresh herbs, such as basil, flat-leaf parsley or mint

3 tbsp olive oil, plus extra for drizzling

2 tomatoes, diced

1 tsp harissa paste

Sea salt and freshly ground black pepper

Peppers and slow cooking go hand in hand – the long, gentle process brings out the best in the taste of the peppers. This is a great recipe for a mid-week supper or as a starter when entertaining.

Using a sharp knife, halve the peppers, attempting to cut along the centre of the stalk so that each half has a piece of stalk attached to it. Carefully remove the seeds, leaving the stalks intact, and arrange the peppers in a single layer in the slow cooker dish (they should fit snugly with few gaps between them). Divide the garlic slices between the peppers.

Place the couscous in a large bowl and add the boiling water. Add the herbs, olive oil, tomatoes and harissa paste, then season with salt and pepper and mix well. Spoon the mixture neatly into the pepper halves and drizzle a little more olive oil over the top. Cover with the lid and cook on high for 1½–2 hours or until the peppers are wonderfully soft but still holding their shape, and the couscous is tender. Serve immediately with some rocket leaves and dollops of Greek yoghurt.

I ALSO LIKE...
to do this with other vegetables, such as halved, hollowed-out courgettes, tomatoes and mini aubergines, using their diced flesh in the couscous stuffing mixture.

WARM TOMATO AND OLIVE CAPONATA

Preparation time: 5 minutes
Cooking time: 4 hours
Serves 6 as an accompaniment
Vegetarian

2 large aubergines, cut into chunks

3 celery sticks, trimmed and finely diced

1 onion, peeled and finely diced

1 tbsp baby capers in brine, drained

75g (3oz) stoned olives

25g (1oz) caster sugar, plus extra to taste

150g (5oz) concentrated tomato purée

4 tbsp red wine vinegar

Sea salt and freshly ground black pepper

3 tbsp cold water

The gentle heat in slow cooking encourages all the wonderful flavours and sweetness out of these ingredients. This dish is rather like an Italian ratatouille and is great with fish and meat as an accompaniment, or as a meal in itself with pasta or a baked potato.

Add the vegetables to the slow cooker dish with the capers, olives, sugar, tomato purée, vinegar, ¼ teaspoon of salt and the water and mix well. Cover with the lid and cook on high for 4 hours or until softened and tender.

Season to taste with more sugar and salt and pepper before serving.

COOKING CONVENTIONALLY?
Cook in an ovenproof casserole dish with a tight-fitting lid for 1 hour in an oven preheated to 170°C (325°F), Gas mark 3.

ROASTED RED PEPPER, TOMATO AND FETA SALAD

Preparation time: 15 minutes
Cooking time: 2–3 hours
Serves 4
Vegetarian

4 red peppers

500g (1lb 2oz) baby cherry tomatoes

1 garlic clove, peeled and finely chopped

Sea salt and freshly ground black pepper

4 handfuls of rocket leaves

200g (7oz) feta cheese, cubed

50g (2oz) toasted pine nuts

Extra virgin olive oil, for drizzling

This salad is packed full of flavour. It is utterly wonderful in the summer, and particularly good for picnics and barbecues, or just as good for brightening up grey days in winter!

Using a sharp knife, deseed the peppers and cut each one into 6 wedges. Add the peppers, tomatoes and garlic to the slow cooker dish and season generously with salt and pepper. Cover with the lid and cook on high for 2–3 hours or until softened.

Mix the rocket leaves into the pepper mixture and season to taste. Spoon the pepper mixture onto a platter, then scatter over the feta and pine nuts. Drizzle with a little olive oil and serve with warmed pitta bread.

I ALSO LIKE...
to let this mixture go cold before tossing it through cooked and cooled pasta to make a perfect summer pasta salad.

MIXED MUSHROOM AND HERB BRUSCHETTA

Mushrooms love being slow cooked! The gentle process seems to maximise their flavour. Use really fresh mushrooms to make the most of their texture and to prevent the mixture from becoming too brown.

Place the mushrooms in the slow cooker dish (you need to have enough to cover the base of the dish thickly). Add the butter, olive oil, 1 teaspoon of salt, lemon zest and juice.

Cut the garlic clove in half lengthways and finely chop one of the pieces. Add this to the mushrooms and mix everything together well. Cover with the lid and cook on low for about 4 hours or until the mushrooms are tender and much of the liquid has evaporated. Stir in the herbs and cheese, then season to taste with salt and pepper.

About 5–10 minutes before the end of cooking, toast the bread until golden, then rub the cut side of the reserved garlic over the toast. Spoon the hot mushroom mixture over the toast and sprinkle with more herbs to garnish.

I ALSO LIKE...
to toss these creamy mushrooms through hot pasta.

Preparation time: 5 minutes
Cooking time: 4 hours
Serves 4
Vegetarian

500g (1lb 2oz) mixed mushrooms, such as button, cup, Portabella or whatever is in season, wiped clean and cut into large wedges or thick slices

50g (2oz) chilled butter, cut into cubes

2 tbsp olive oil

Sea salt and freshly ground black pepper

Finely grated zest and juice of 1 lemon (preferably unwaxed)

1 garlic clove, peeled

4 tbsp finely chopped fresh herbs, such as parsley, basil, mint and chives, plus extra to garnish

50g (2oz) creamy Italian cheese, such as Taleggio or Dolcelatte, crumbled

8 bruschetta slices or slices of ciabatta

BALSAMIC BEETROOT AND ORANGE SALAD

Preparation time: 10 minutes

Cooking time: 4–5 hours

Serves 4

Vegetarian

---

4 raw beetroots, scrubbed

---

1 garlic clove, peeled and crushed

---

3 oranges

50ml (1¾fl oz) balsamic vinegar

50ml (1¾fl oz) extra virgin olive oil

A small handful of fresh mint leaves

---

1 tbsp finely diced shallot

Sea salt and freshly ground black pepper

150g (5oz) mixed salad leaves, such as lamb's lettuce or baby leaves

---

200g (7oz) soft goat's cheese, crumbled

50g (2oz) walnut pieces

This classic combination of flavours is always a winner in our house.

Trim the roots and green leafy tops from the beetroot, cut them into chunky wedges and place into the slow cooker dish together with the garlic, finely grated zest and juice from one of the oranges, the vinegar and half the olive oil. Cover with the lid and cook on low for 4–5 hours or until tender. Leave to cool completely in the slow cooker.

Using a serrated knife, cut the top and bottom from the remaining oranges. Place them on a board and slice off the peel in downward strips, being careful to remove the pith as well. Then hold one orange in your hand over a small bowl and cut each segment of orange away by cutting between the membranes. Allow the segments and any juice to collect in the bowl.

Finely shred half of the mint leaves. Add the remaining olive oil, chopped mint, shallot and salt and pepper to the orange segments and set aside.

Place the salad leaves on a large platter. Using a slotted spoon, remove the beetroot from its cooking liquid and scatter over the salad. Drizzle over the orange segments and dressing, then scatter with the remaining mint, the goat's cheese and walnuts to serve.

COOKING CONVENTIONALLY?
Wrap the prepared beetroot in foil and cook in an oven preheated to 180°C (350°F), Gas mark 4, for 2–3 hours or until tender.

SKATE WINGS WITH WARM CITRUS AND TOMATO SALAD

Preparation time: 10 minutes

Cooking time: 2 hours

Serves 2

6 mixed tomatoes (use different colours, sizes and shapes), thickly sliced

1 red chilli, deseeded and chopped

½ red onion, peeled and very finely sliced

1 tsp red wine vinegar

Finely grated zest and juice of 1 lemon (preferably unwaxed)

Finely grated zest and juice of 1 orange

Sea salt and freshly ground black pepper

2 tbsp cold water

2 skate wings, about 400g (14oz) each

2 tbsp finely chopped fresh mint leaves

1 tbsp finely chopped fresh basil

Extra virgin olive oil, for drizzling

This is a fantastically flavoursome dish. It works really well with other white fish too like plaice, John Dory, cod or haddock.

Place the tomatoes in the slow cooker dish, then sprinkle with the chilli, onion, vinegar, lemon and orange zests. Season with salt and pepper, add the cold water and mix well.

Arrange the fish on top of the tomatoes in a single layer if possible, but don't worry if not. Cover with the lid and cook on low for 2 hours or until the fish is tender when tested with the tip of a knife.

Drizzle the lemon and orange juice over the fish and carefully place onto warm serving plates. Sprinkle the herbs over the tomatoes and then spoon onto the plates with the fish. Drizzle with extra virgin olive oil and serve with new potatoes and watercress.

PEPPERED MACKEREL, NEW POTATO AND CAPER SALAD WITH LEMON DRESSING

Slow cooking these ingredients together ensures that their flavours intensify and marry in the most wonderful way.

Cook the potatoes a saucepan of boiling water for 5 minutes, then drain thoroughly and tip into the slow cooker dish.

Add the capers, olive oil and 2 teaspoons of the lemon juice and mix everything together.

Break the mackerel into large pieces and place on top of the potatoes. Cover with the lid and cook on high for 1½ hours or until the potatoes are tender. Remove the lid and add the remaining lemon juice. Check the seasoning and add salt and pepper, if necessary.

Place the salad leaves on two serving plates and spoon the mackerel and potatoes over the top, drizzle the warm juices over to make a dressing and eat straight away.

COOKING CONVENTIONALLY?
Place in a baking dish, cover with foil and cook in an oven preheated to 160°C (325°F), Gas mark 3 for 1½ hours or until the potatoes are tender.

Preparation time: **10 minutes**
Cooking time: **1½ hours**
Serves **2**

225g (8oz) baby new potatoes, cut in half lengthways

1 tbsp capers in brine, drained (or use salted capers but rinse and drain very well before use)

1 tbsp extra virgin olive oil

Juice of 1 lemon

200g (7oz) smoked peppered mackerel fillets, skin removed

Sea salt and freshly ground black pepper (optional)

100g (3½oz) mixed salad leaves

BRAISED CHICORY WITH PARMESAN

Preparation time: 5 minutes
Cooking time: 2 hours 5 minutes
Serves 4

4 heads chicory

Juice of 1 lemon

25g (1oz) butter, melted

1 tbsp wholegrain mustard

1 tsp golden caster sugar

4 tbsp freshly grated Parmesan cheese (optional)

Slow cooking chicory makes it really soft. Here, it is topped with Parmesan and cooked until the cheese forms a lovely golden crust.

Using a sharp knife, cut the chicory in half lengthways, then cut out the thick white stem and discard.

Place the chicory in a large bowl, pour over the lemon juice and turn the chicory until it is completely coated in the juice. This will stop the chicory going brown. Arrange the chicory in the slow cooker dish in a single layer cut side down and pour any remaining lemon juice over the top.

Mix the melted butter, mustard and sugar together and drizzle over the chicory. Cover with the lid and cook on high for 2 hours.

If your slow cooker dish is flameproof (see manufacturer's instructions), preheat the grill to its highest setting. Carefully turn the chicory halves over and sprinkle with the Parmesan cheese (if not, transfer to a shallow oven dish before grilling). Place under the hot grill for 3–5 minutes or until golden and bubbling. Serve immediately with salad and crusty bread.

COOKING CONVENTIONALLY?
Place in a ovenproof baking dish, cover with a tight-fitting lid or foil and cook in an oven preheated to 180°C (350°F), Gas mark 4 for 1–2 hours or until tender.

CHORIZO IN SHERRY AND TOMATO SAUCE

This is a wonderful tapas dish or just as good as a starter – try it spooned onto toasted bruschetta.

Turn the slow cooker on to its highest setting. Place the chorizo and garlic in the slow cooker dish, cover with the lid and leave to cook for 30 minutes or until the chorizo has started to leach its orange, paprika-coloured oil.

Meanwhile, cook the potatoes in a saucepan of salted boiling water over a high heat for 5 minutes or until just becoming tender. Drain and set aside.

Add the cherry tomatoes to the slow cooker dish together with the potatoes, sherry and sugar. Mix well, cover with the lid and leave to cook for a further 2 hours. Season to taste with salt and pepper and mix in the parsley. Serve hot with crusty bread to mop up the sauce.

COOKING CONVENTIONALLY?
If you want to use the oven? Omit the first step and place the par-boiled potatoes and the other remaining ingredients into a large baking dish, cover with a tight-fitting lid or foil and cook in an oven preheated to 180°C (350°F), Gas mark 4 for 1–2 hours or until the potatoes are tender.

Preparation time: 10 minutes
Cooking time: 2½ hours
Serves 4 as a light, tapas-style lunch or starter

200g (7oz) chorizo sausage, thickly sliced

2 garlic cloves, peeled and finely sliced

250g (9oz) baby new potatoes, washed and cut into thick slices

400g (14oz) cherry tomatoes, halved

2 tbsp dry fino sherry

1 tsp caster sugar

Sea salt and freshly ground black pepper

2 tbsp roughly chopped fresh flat-leaf parsley

STICKY ORANGE AND SESAME CHICKEN DRUMSTICKS

Preparation time: 12 minutes
Cooking time: 6 hours 10 minutes
Serves **4**

8 chicken drumsticks

**Finely grated zest and juice of
1 large orange**

2 tbsp dark muscovado sugar

2 tsp Chinese five-spice powder

**2 tbsp Japanese teriyaki sauce or
dark soy sauce**

1 tbsp toasted sesame oil

1 tbsp sesame seeds, to garnish

**These tender pieces of chicken are coated in a glossy glaze that
is full of flavour. You can also use chicken wings or thighs.**

Warm a large non-stick frying pan over a high heat. When hot,
add the chicken drumsticks and cook for 10 minutes until golden.
Place the chicken in the slow cooker dish.

Sprinkle the orange zest over the chicken and pour in the juice.
Add all the remaining ingredients except the sesame seeds and
carefully mix everything together until the chicken is coated in
the sauce. Cover with the lid and cook on low for 6 hours or until
the chicken is thoroughly cooked and piping hot.

Spoon the chicken onto a large serving plate and scatter the
sesame seeds over the top. Serve drizzled with cooking juices
with freshly cooked egg noodles or rice and stir-fried vegetables.

LIVER AND BACON

Preparation time: 15 minutes
Cooking time: 6–8 hours
Serves **4**

1 tbsp olive oil

**4 rashers smoked streaky bacon,
diced**

2 onions, peeled and finely sliced

500g (1lb 2oz) lamb's liver portions

2 tbsp plain flour

**Sea salt and freshly ground black
pepper**

500ml (18fl oz) red wine

2 fresh thyme sprigs

2 bay leaves

**A school lunch classic that seems to be as polarising now as it
ever was! However, this simple casserole is well worth trying
even if you're not a liver fan; if you are, you'll love it.**

Warm the olive oil in a large frying pan over a medium heat.
When hot, add the bacon and fry briefly before adding the
onions. Cook for about 5 minutes or until golden and softened
slightly. Spoon into the slow cooker dish.

Return the pan to the heat. Place the liver, flour and seasoning
into a freezer bag, seal and toss quickly to coat. Add the liver
to the hot pan and sear for about 1 minute on each side or until
browned. Add to the slow cooker dish.

Pour in the wine and add the herbs. Cover with the lid and cook
on low for 6–8 hours or until the liver is tender and the sauce
is thickened. Serve with buttered jacket potatoes and seasonal
vegetables.

COOKING CONVENTIONALLY?
Follow the recipe through steps 1 and 2, then place in a casserole
dish, cover with a tight-fitting lid or foil and cook in an oven
preheated to 170°C (325°F), Gas mark 3 for 1–2 hours.

EASY CHICKEN LIVER PÂTÉ

Preparation time: 10 minutes
Cooking time: 2¼ hours
Makes 500g (1lb 2oz) pâté

400g (14oz) fresh chicken livers, rinsed and drained

1 tbsp butter, plus extra for greasing

1 small onion, peeled and finely diced

50g (2oz) dried natural breadcrumbs

2 tbsp double cream

2 tbsp Marsala or brandy (optional)

125g (4½oz) pork mince

2 fresh sage leaves

1 fresh thyme sprig, leaves only

A small pinch of mace

Sea salt and freshly ground black pepper

I'm a real fan of chicken liver pâté, and it's so economical to make! I like a smooth pâté, but if you prefer, simply process for less time to make a coarse version. This pâté will keep in the fridge for about a week and also freezes really well for a month.

Pick over the livers, trimming any membranes away. Butter a small loaf tin or ovenproof dish that will fit into your slow cooker dish.

Melt the remaining butter in a frying pan over a medium heat. Add the onion and sweat for about 5 minutes or until soft. Remove from the heat and add the breadcrumbs, cream and Marsala or brandy. Set aside for about 5 minutes.

Place the onion, soaked breadcrumbs and all the other ingredients except for one of the sage leaves in a food processor and blitz until it reaches your preferred consistency. Place one of the sage leaves, attractive side down, into the bottom of the prepared tin or dish, then spoon the pâté mixture over the top, season with some salt and pepper and level the surface. Cover with a double layer of buttered foil.

Place the tin or dish in the slow cooker dish and carefully pour enough boiling water around the outside to come about one-third of the way up the sides of the tin or dish. Cover with the lid and cook on high for about 2 hours or until firm to the touch. Remove the tin or dish from the slow cooker and leave to cool completely before unwrapping and turning out. Cut into slices and serve with hot toast.

FARMHOUSE PÂTÉ

Try this rustic pâté served with crusty bread and pickles.

Line a non-stick 1kg (2lb 4oz) loaf tin with 6 bacon rashers, placing them next to each other horizontally so that the ends of the bacon overhang each side of the tin and the base is completely covered.

Roughly chop 3 of the remaining bacon rashers and 300g (10oz) of the chicken livers and place them in a large mixing bowl. Add the mince and mix well with your hands until the mince is very smooth. Mix in the herbs, the shallots, 2 teaspoons of salt, the brandy and egg.

Spoon half of the mixture into the tin and press down into the corners with the back of a spoon. Place the remaining chicken livers in a single layer over the top and season with some salt and pepper. Cover with the remaining mince mixture and press down again. Cut the remaining bacon rashers in half and lay them horizontally across the base of the terrine, then fold the overhanging ends of bacon over the top to seal everything in neatly. Cover tightly with a layer of parchment paper then foil.

Place the tin in the slow cooker and carefully pour enough boiling water around the outside to come halfway up the sides of the tin. Cover with the lid and cook on high for 3–4 hours or until the mixture is firm and the juices run clear when tested with the tip of a knife. Remove the tin from the slow cooker and leave to cool slightly before unwrapping. Drain off any excess fat, then leave to cool completely. Serve in thick slices.

Preparation time: 20 minutes
Cooking time: 3–4 hours
Makes 1kg (2lb 4oz) terrine (about 10 slices)

12 rashers smoked streaky bacon

400g (14oz) chicken livers, rinsed

500g (1lb 2oz) pork mince

1 tbsp finely chopped fresh flat-leaf parsley

1 tbsp finely chopped fresh thyme leaves

½ tbsp finely chopped fresh sage leaves

2 shallots, peeled and finely diced

Sea salt and freshly ground black pepper

2 tbsp brandy

1 large egg, beaten

DUCK CONFIT WITH SUGARED PISTACHIO, ORANGE AND POMEGRANATE SALAD

Preparation time: 10 minutes, plus chilling

Cooking time: 2 hours

Serves 4

4 free-range duck legs

Sea salt and freshly ground black pepper

4 fresh thyme sprigs

50g (2oz) pistachios

1 tbsp golden caster sugar

200g (7oz) mixed baby salad leaves

2 spring onions, trimmed and finely shredded

1 pomegranate, halved

1 orange, cut into segments

Extra virgin olive oil, for drizzling

This dish looks great, tastes great, and is great!

Rub the duck legs with 4 tablespoons of salt. Cover and place in the fridge for at least 1 hour. Dry the legs with kitchen paper, removing excess salt.

Place the thyme in the slow cooker dish and rest the duck legs on top. Cover with the lid and cook on low for 2 hours or until the duck is bathing in a pool of its own fat. Put the duck into a shallow dish together with the herbs and pour the liquid fat over the top to cover the duck completely. Leave to cool, then cover and chill until needed. It will keep for 2–3 days.

Thirty minutes before eating, remove the duck from the fridge. Put the pistachios and sugar in a small heavy-based saucepan and place over a high heat for 1–2 minutes until the sugar has just melted. Remove from the heat and stir to roughly coat the nuts in the caramel. Allow to cool, then roughly chop. Place the salad and onions on a large platter. Using a fork, release the seeds from the pomegranate, discarding any of the bitter white membrane. Scatter the seeds and orange segments over the salad.

Remove the duck from the now solidified fat and scrape off all the fat and skin. Using 2 forks, shred the flesh into bite-sized pieces and scatter the meat over the salad. Drizzle with a little olive oil, add seasoning to taste and scatter with the sugared pistachios. Serve straight away.

CREAMY BEETROOT SOUP

Beetroot makes a great soup, but when it's slow-cooked first it's even better! Serve with crusty bread.

Place the beetroot, potato and onion in the slow cooker dish. Add the caraway seeds, stock and salt and pepper and mix well.

Cover with the lid and cook on high for 4 hours or until the beetroot is completely tender. Pour the mixture into a food processor and blitz until smooth, adding extra hot stock if it is too thick and needs thinning down.

Spoon all but a few spoonfuls of the crème fraîche into the soup and blitz again to combine. Season to taste.

Ladle the soup into individual bowls immediately and eat warm or leave to cool completely and chill before serving. Hot or cold, serve topped with a dollop of the remaining crème fraîche and a few extra caraway seeds sprinkled over.

TRY...
For a lighter alternative, simply omit the crème fraîche.

Preparation time: 15 minutes
Cooking time: 4 hours
Serves 4
Vegetarian

4 fresh raw beetroot, about 450g (1lb) in total, peeled and diced

1 potato, about 100g (3½oz), peeled and diced

1 onion, peeled and diced

1 tsp caraway seeds, plus extra to serve

1 litre (1¾ pints) hot vegetable stock, plus extra if needed

Sea salt and freshly ground black pepper

200ml (7fl oz) crème fraîche

BUTTERNUT AND CHILLI SOUP

Making this simple soup will easily fit in around your busy lifestyle. Prepare the squash and relax while it cooks. Then when you're ready to eat, simply boil the kettle, make up the stock, blitz it with the squash and you have lunch ready to go!

Place the squash in the slow cooker dish. Reserve 4 small pinches of chilli for the garnish and add the rest to the slow cooker dish together with the onion and garlic. Season generously with salt and pepper and add the olive oil.

Cover with the lid and cook on high for 4 hours or until the squash is very tender. Spoon the mixture into a food processor (you may need to do this in batches) and add the stock. Blitz until smooth and season to taste.

Ladle the soup into warm bowls, dot with a few coriander leaves and sprinkle with the reserved chilli to serve.

FAB FOR THE FREEZER
Make a double batch and freeze some for a busy day.

Preparation time: 10 Minutes
Cooking time: 4 Hours
Serves 4
Vegetarian

1 large butternut squash, about 1kg (2lb 4oz), peeled, deseeded and cut into chunks

1 large red chilli, deseeded and diced

1 red onion, peeled and diced

2 garlic cloves, peeled and diced

Sea salt and freshly ground black pepper

1 tbsp olive oil

1 litre (1¾ pints) hot vegetable stock

Fresh coriander leaves, to garnish

SPINACH AND LENTIL SOUP

Preparation time: 15 minutes
Cooking time: 3–4 hours
Serves 4

75g (3oz) brown or green lentils

Olive oil

1 garlic clove, peeled

1 red onion, peeled and finely diced

1 celery stick, trimmed and finely diced

1 x 400g (14oz) tin chopped tomatoes

2 fresh thyme sprigs

1 bay leaf, broken

2 litres (3½ pints) stock

125g (4½oz) baby spinach leaves

Sea salt and freshly ground black pepper

Extra virgin olive oil or basil oil, for drizzling

This colourful, hearty soup is packed with flavour. You can use either chicken or vegetarian stock.

Wash the lentils in cold water and drain thoroughly. Pour in 1–2mm (¹⁄₁₆in) of olive oil to cover the base of the slow cooker dish.

Using your thumb, press the garlic firmly to bruise it, then add it to the dish. Add the lentils and mix to coat in the oil. Add the onion, celery, tomatoes and herbs and mix together. Don't season the soup at this stage, as salt will toughen the lentils. Pour the stock over the lentils. Cover with the lid and cook on high for 3–4 hours or until the lentils are tender.

Using a slotted spoon, remove the garlic and herbs. Mix the spinach into the soup and stir until the leaves are just wilted. Season to taste with salt and pepper.

Ladle the soup into warm bowls and drizzle with a touch of extra virgin olive oil or basil oil before serving with ciabatta.

FAB FOR THE FREEZER
Leave to cool before transferring to freezerproof containers and freezing for up to three months. Defrost thoroughly before reheating gently on the hob (never in the slow cooker).

SPICY CELERIAC AND APPLE SOUP

Preparation time: 10 minutes
Cooking time: 4 hours
Serves 6
Vegetarian

1 large celeriac, about 1.5kg (3lb 5oz), peeled (about 1.3kg/2lb 13oz peeled weight) and cut into 3cm (1¼in) chunks

1 large onion, peeled and cut into 3cm (1¼in) chunks

1 cooking apple, peeled, cored and diced

Juice of 1 lemon

2 vegetable stock cubes

1 tbsp medium curry paste

1 litre (1¾ pints) boiling water

Sea salt and freshly ground black pepper

I absolutely love celeriac raw in salads and remoulade, but here it really benefits from long slow cooking, which coaxes out its characteristic nutty flavour. The warming spices of the curry paste and the tart apple also work well to complete this easy soup. You can also make this with parsnips instead of celeriac.

Place the celeriac and onion chunks in the slow cooker dish. Add the diced apple, then pour over the lemon juice and toss together until everything is coated in the juice.

Place the stock cubes and curry paste into a large measuring jug, then pour over the boiling water and stir to dissolve the cubes. Pour this mixture over the celeriac and top up with more boiling water if the vegetables and apple are not covered with liquid (otherwise the apple will turn brown). Cover with the lid and cook on high for 4 hours or until the vegetables are completely tender.

Remove the slow cooker dish from the heated base and place it on a heatproof surface. Blitz the soup with a hand-held blender until completely smooth (or blend in batches in a food processor). Add more hot stock if you like your soup thinner. Season to taste with salt and pepper and serve.

SPLIT PEA AND HAM SOUP

Preparation time: 5 minutes, plus overnight soaking
Cooking time: 2–3 hours
Serves 4

2 tbsp olive oil

2 leeks, white part only, diced

2 garlic cloves, peeled and finely chopped

500g (1lb 2oz) green split peas, soaked overnight and drained

2 litres (3½ pints) chicken or vegetable stock

2 tbsp roughly chopped fresh flat-leaf parsley

50g (2oz) ham, finely shredded

This easy soup is very warming and tasty – perfect for a cold day or if you're in need of some real comfort food.

Pour the olive oil into the slow cooker dish, then mix in the leeks, garlic, drained split peas and stock.

Cover with the lid and cook on high for 1 hour. Remove the lid and skim off and discard any froth from the surface with a slotted spoon. Mix the soup well, then cover again and cook for a further 1–2 hours or until the peas are tender.

Ladle the soup into serving bowls and top with the parsley and shredded ham. Serve with hot buttered toast.

I ALSO LIKE...
replacing the ham with hot, crispy bacon pieces.

CHICKEN AND LEMON SOUP

Slow cooking the chicken on the bone before adding it to the soup gives it a wonderful flavour.

Place the chicken wings, celery, leek, garlic, thyme and lemon zest and juice into the slow cooker dish and mix well. Cover with the lid and cook on high for 2 hours, stirring halfway through cooking.

After 2 hours, carefully pour enough boiling water into the slow cooker dish to cover the chicken and stir to combine. Cover with the lid again and cook on low for a further 4–6 hours (the longer the better).

Strain the chicken and vegetables through a sieve into a large saucepan. Pick over the chicken, discarding any skin or bone but saving the meat, and add the meat to the pan. Bring to the boil over a high heat, skimming with a slotted spoon to remove any remaining skin, sinew or bits of vegetable that have escaped the straining process.

Add the potato to the soup and simmer for 10 minutes or until the potato is tender. Remove the pan from the heat and stir in the cream. Season to taste with salt and pepper and serve immediately sprinkled with a few lemon thyme leaves.

I ALSO LIKE...

to use baby pasta or risoni (a type of pasta that looks like large grains of rice, used in soups, salads, stews, stuffings, etc.) instead of potato in this soup.

Preparation time: 5 minutes
Cooking time: 6½–8½ hours
Serves 4

750g (1lb 10oz) chicken wings

1 celery stick, trimmed and finely diced

1 leek, trimmed and finely diced

1 garlic clove, peeled and crushed

1 fresh lemon thyme sprig, plus extra to garnish (or use 1 ordinary thyme sprig)

Finely grated zest and juice of 1 lemon (preferably unwaxed)

1 large potato, peeled and cut into small 1cm (½in) cubes

3 tbsp double cream

Sea salt and freshly ground black pepper

SPICY SEAFOOD CHOWDER

Preparation time: 10 minutes
Cooking time: 2¼ hours
Serves 4

4 rashers smoked streaky bacon, diced

4 tbsp dry vermouth

1 small onion, peeled and finely diced

2 celery sticks, trimmed and cut into 5mm (¼in) pieces

250g (9oz) floury potatoes, peeled and diced into 1cm (½in) cubes

2 corn on the cob

2 bay leaves, broken

500ml (18fl oz) chicken or vegetable stock

2 red chillies, deseeded and finely diced

3 tbsp crème fraîche

250g (9oz) mixed ready-to-eat, cooked seafood, such as prawns, calamari or mussels

1 tbsp chopped fresh dill

A hearty soup with just enough spice to give your taste buds a bit of a kick. If you don't like spicy food, then either add more crème fraîche or simply less chilli.

Warm a frying pan over a medium heat. When hot, add the bacon and stir-fry for about 5 minutes or until opaque but not coloured. Add the vermouth and remove the pan from the heat. Stir well, scraping any caramelised bacon from the base of the pan, pour into the slow cooker dish, then add the onion, celery and potatoes to the slow cooker dish.

Stand the corn on their ends and carefully run a knife from top to bottom to cut off the kernels. Add to the slow cooker dish together with the bay leaves and stock.

Place half of the chillies in the slow cooker dish and set the rest aside. Cover with the lid and cook on high for 2 hours or until the potato is tender.

Ladle half of the chowder into a food processor and blitz until smooth. Return the purée to the slow cooker dish and mix in. Add the crème fraîche, seafood and the remaining chillies and mix to combine. Cover again and leave for 15 minutes to heat through thoroughly. Serve immediately in warm bowls, sprinkled with chopped dill.

VIETNAMESE BEEF 'PHO' BROTH

This is a substantial meal in a bowl. It's a nice idea to assemble this dish at the dining table – serve a bowl of noodles and then a selection platter with bean sprouts, spring onions and more sliced chilli for example – and let people customise their own broth.

Place the steak strips in the slow cooker dish and top with the chilli, ginger, garlic, cloves (if using) and stock. Make sure that the meat is completely immersed in the stock. Cover with the lid and cook on low for 8–10 hours or until the meat is wonderfully tender.

When you're ready to eat, place the noodles in a large bowl and cover with boiling water. Leave to stand for 4 minutes. Drain thoroughly, then divide among 4 deep serving bowls. Top each one with a handful of bean sprouts, some spring onion, chopped coriander and mint.

Season the hot stock with the lime juice and fish sauce to taste. Top the noodles with the cooked beef and then ladle over the hot stock. Garnish with a few whole mint and coriander leaves. Serve immediately with lime wedges to squeeze over.

Preparation time: 5 minutes
Cooking time: 8–10 hours
Serves 4

400g (14oz) beef feather steak (available from good butchers) or braising steak, sliced into thin strips

1 red chilli, sliced

1 tsp shredded fresh root ginger

1 garlic clove, peeled and left whole

6 cloves (optional)

1.3 litres (2¼ pints) cold good-quality beef stock

250g (9oz) vermicelli (fine rice noodles)

100g (3½oz) bean sprouts

4 spring onions, trimmed and finely shredded

4 tbsp roughly chopped coriander leaves, plus some whole

4 tbsp roughly chopped mint leaves, plus some whole

Juice of 1 lime, to taste

1 tbsp fish sauce, to taste

Lime wedges, to serve

BREAKFAST OMELETTE

Preparation time: **5 minutes**
Cooking time: **6–9 hours**
Serves **6**

50g (2oz) butter, diced and softened

650g (1lb 7oz) potatoes, such as King Edward or Maris Piper, unpeeled and diced into 1cm (½in) cubes

12 rashers smoked back bacon, diced

1 onion, peeled and diced

12 eggs

250ml (9fl oz) skimmed milk

½ tsp mustard powder

Sea salt and freshly ground black pepper

This recipe caters for a larger number, so making breakfast for a crowd is a doddle.

Butter the inside of the slow cooker dish very thoroughly with about one-third of the butter, then arrange a layer of the diced potatoes in the base of the dish.

Working quickly so that the potatoes don't have a chance to turn brown, cover the potatoes with a layer of bacon and a layer of onion.

In a large mixing bowl, whisk the eggs, milk and mustard powder together. Season to taste with salt and pepper and pour the mixture into the slow cooker dish. Dot the remaining butter over the top.

Cover with the lid and cook on low overnight or for up to 9 hours until set in the centre.

Remove from the slow cooker base and leave to stand for 5 minutes before cutting into wedges or squares and serving with plenty of crusty bread and grilled cherry tomatoes.

I ALSO LIKE...
adding diced black pudding or chorizo with the diced bacon.

PASTA, RICE
+
GRAINS

CARAMELISED SWEET AND SOUR SESAME SHALLOTS WITH NOODLES

Preparation time: 10 minutes

Cooking time: 2 hours

Serves 4

Vegetarian

10–12 shallots

100ml (3½fl oz) red wine vinegar

2 tbsp tomato purée

2 tbsp toasted sesame oil

2 tbsp soft dark brown sugar

2 tbsp toasted sesame seeds

Fresh coriander leaves, to garnish

When onions and shallots are slow-cooked they deserve to be a main ingredient in their own right! Here, they are cooked in a sweet and sour sauce until they caramelise and become meltingly tender and full of flavour.

Using a sharp knife, halve the shallots lengthways and then peel – it's much easier doing it this way, rather than peeling them first. Place the shallot halves in the slow cooker dish.

In a measuring jug, mix the wine vinegar, tomato purée, sesame oil and sugar together. Pour over the shallots and mix well to combine. Ensure that the shallots are nestled together in a single layer.

Cover and cook on high for 1 hour before carefully turning the shallots over. Cover again and cook for a further hour or until the shallots are tender and caramelised.

Scatter over the sesame seeds and toss to combine. Garnish with coriander and serve with freshly cooked egg noodles.

COOKING CONVENTIONALLY?
Place in an ovenproof dish and cook, uncovered, in an oven preheated to 180°C (350°F), Gas mark 4, turning occasionally, for 1–2 hours or until soft and caramelised.

CREAMY ROASTED GARLIC AND ROCKET PASTA SAUCE

Preparation time: 2 minutes
Cooking time: 2½–3 hours, plus cooking the pasta
Serves 4
Vegetarian

1 whole head of garlic, unpeeled

100ml (3½fl oz) white wine

8 tbsp double cream

1 egg yolk

Sea salt and freshly ground black pepper

400g (14oz) dried pasta, such as farfalle or fusilli

50g (2oz) rocket leaves

Slow cooking garlic makes it sweet and flavoursome – perfect in a creamy pasta dish like this.

Place the whole garlic in the slow cooker dish and pour the wine over the top. Cover with the lid and cook on low for 2½–3 hours, adding more wine if it starts to boil dry, until the garlic is soft.

Cut the top from the garlic to expose the tips of the cloves. Squeeze out the flesh into a bowl and mash until smooth. Add the cream together with any juices from the slow cooker dish, then beat in the egg yolk. Season to taste with salt and pepper.

Bring a large saucepan of salted water to the boil. Add the pasta and cook according to the packet instructions or until firm to the bite. Drain the pasta, leaving a little of the cooking water (about 2 tablespoons) behind in the pan. Return the drained pasta to the pan and add the garlic sauce and rocket. Fold through quickly (to avoid making scrambled egg!) and season to taste. Serve with a tomato and red onion salad.

EASY TOMATO PASTA SAUCE

Preparation time: 5 minutes
Cooking time: 8–12 hours
Serves 4
Vegetarian

2 x 400g (14oz) tins chopped tomatoes

1 small onion, peeled and finely diced

2 garlic cloves, peeled and crushed

1 tsp dried oregano

1 tsp sea salt

1 tbsp caster sugar

100ml (3½fl oz) red wine

60ml (2fl oz) extra virgin olive oil

Fresh basil leaves, torn, to garnish

Freshly grated Parmesan cheese, to serve

There still seems to be a certain suggestion that tinned food is inferior to fresh. When it comes to cooking with tomatoes, and especially tomato sauce, tinned tomatoes are the way to go!

Place the tomatoes, onion, garlic, oregano, salt, sugar and wine into the slow cooker dish. Drizzle over half of the olive oil and mix well.

Cover with the lid and cook on low for 8 hours or for up to 12 hours.

Season with more salt to taste and mix in the remaining olive oil. Spoon over hot, freshly cooked pasta and sprinkle with torn basil leaves and grated Parmesan to serve.

I ALSO LIKE...
to add a whole dried chilli to the sauce at the start of cooking for an extra kick. Remove it before serving.

ITALIAN TOMATO AND AUBERGINE SAUCE

One of my lasting memories of Sicily was the classic sugo alla Norma (tomato and aubergine sauce). This is my version.

Warm a large frying pan over a high heat. When hot, add the olive oil, onion and garlic and cook for 5 minutes or until softened but not coloured. Transfer to the slow cooker dish.

Stir the pepper and aubergine chunks into the slow cooker dish with the tomatoes, capers, wine, oregano and seasoning to taste. Cover with the lid and cook for 6–8 hours or until rich and thick.

Taste and add more seasoning if necessary, and drizzle with extra olive oil to taste. Add the cooked drained pasta to the slow cooker dish and mix well. Scatter with the basil leaves and serve with plenty of ricotta (if using) and freshly ground black pepper.

I ALSO LIKE...
to make this dish and then spoon it into a baking dish, before topping with lots of ricotta and Parmesan cheese and baking in an oven preheated to 190°C (375°F), Gas mark 5, until golden and crisp.

Preparation time: 10 minutes
Cooking time: 6¼–8¼ hours
Serves 4
Vegetarian

1 tbsp olive oil, plus extra to serve

1 small onion, peeled and chopped

1 garlic clove, peeled and crushed

1 green pepper, deseeded and cut into 2cm (¾in) chunks

2 large aubergines, about 450g (1lb), trimmed and cut into 2cm (¾in) chunks

1 x 400g (14oz) tin chopped tomatoes

1 tbsp baby capers, rinsed and drained

100ml (3½fl oz) red wine

1 tsp dried oregano

Sea salt and freshly ground black pepper

150–200g (5–7oz) freshly cooked penne pasta

A large handful of fresh basil leaves

Ricotta cheese, to serve (optional)

PUMPKIN AND PARMESAN PASTA SAUCE

Preparation time: 10 minutes
**Cooking time: 3–4 hours, plus
cooking the pasta**
Serves 4

1 orange-fleshed pumpkin or
butternut squash, peeled, deseeded
and diced into 2cm (¾in) chunks

1 onion, peeled and finely diced

1 red chilli, deseeded and finely
diced

1 garlic clove, peeled and crushed

2 tbsp olive oil

¼ tsp ground nutmeg, plus extra
to taste

Sea salt and freshly ground black
and white pepper

2 tbsp double cream

3 tbsp freshly grated Parmesan
cheese

100ml (3½fl oz) hot vegetable stock

350–400g (12–14oz) penne pasta

1 tbsp roughly chopped fresh
flat-leaf parsley leaves

*This creamy pasta sauce is so easy and economical to make.
I love it tossed through pasta, but it also works well as a side
dish.*

Place the pumpkin or squash, onion, chilli, garlic and olive oil into
the slow cooker dish together with the nutmeg and some salt and
white pepper. Cover with the lid and cook on low for 3–4 hours or
until softened.

Place the contents of the slow cooker dish into a food processor,
add the cream and two-thirds of the Parmesan cheese and blitz
until smooth, gradually drizzling in the hot stock as the motor is
running. Season to taste and add more nutmeg if required.

Meanwhile, cook and drain the pasta according to the instructions
on the packet. Toss the sauce with the hot pasta and sprinkle
over the remaining Parmesan cheese and the chopped parsley.
Serve with plenty of freshly ground black pepper.

I ALSO LIKE...
to vary this recipe to make a risotto. Cook the pumpkin to the
end of paragraph 1, add 350g (12oz) risotto rice and 1.5 litres
(2½ pints) vegetable stock, cover and cook on low for 1½–2 hours,
without stirring or uncovering, until tender.

MARINARA TOMATO AND SEAFOOD PASTA SAUCE

This easy sauce is a great store-cupboard standby in our house as I usually have prawns or mixed seafood in the freezer and always have a cupboard full of the other ingredients. Always defrost the seafood thoroughly before using.

Place the tomatoes, onion, garlic, salt, sugar and wine in the slow cooker dish. Drizzle over half of the olive oil and mix well. Cover with the lid and cook on low for 8–12 hours or until rich and thick.

Increase the heat to high, stir in the seafood, cover again and cook for a further 30 minutes or until piping hot.

Taste and add more seasoning if necessary, and mix in the remaining olive oil. Spoon over hot, freshly cooked pasta, such as spaghetti or tagliatelle, then sprinkle over basil leaves to serve.

I ALSO LIKE...
to add a whole dried chilli to the sauce at the start of cooking for a spicy kick..

Preparation time: 5 minutes
Cooking time: 8½–12½ hours
Serves **4**

2 x 400g (14oz) tins chopped tomatoes

1 small onion, peeled and finely diced

2 garlic cloves, peeled and crushed

1 tsp sea salt

1 tbsp caster sugar

100ml (3½fl oz) white wine

60ml (2fl oz) extra virgin olive oil

400g (14oz) mixed cooked seafood

Freshly cooked pasta, to serve

Fresh basil leaves, to serve

PRESERVED LEMON AND PINE NUT QUINOA WITH SUN-DRIED TOMATO SAUCE

Preparation time: 10 minutes
Cooking time: 3 hours, plus cooking the pasta
Serves 4
Vegetarian

6 preserved lemons (see page 187)

1 large onion, peeled, halved and cut into 1cm (½in) wedges

1 red chilli, deseeded and finely chopped

1 tbsp olive oil

1 tsp golden caster sugar

Sea salt and freshly ground black pepper

200g (7oz) quinoa

500ml (18fl oz) hot vegetable stock

50g (2oz) pine nuts

8 tbsp fresh coriander leaves

4 tbsp sun-dried tomato paste

8 tbsp boiling water

Quinoa (pronounced keen-wah) is a grain from South America now widely available in supermarkets. It is not dissimilar in texture to couscous and has an appealing nutty flavour.

Cut the preserved lemons into quarters, then remove and discard the flesh. Shred the lemon skins into strips. Place the onion, strips of lemon skin, the chilli, olive oil and sugar in the slow cooker dish and season to taste with salt and pepper. Cover with the lid and cook on high for 2 hours or until the onion is very soft.

Add the quinoa and hot stock and mix well to combine. Cover again and cook for a further hour.

Meanwhile, warm a frying pan over a medium heat. When hot, add the pine nuts and cook for 3–5 minutes, shaking the pan frequently, until they are an even golden colour. Remove from the heat and set aside.

When the quinoa is tender, with just a little bite to it (like cooked rice or couscous), stir in the coriander and the reserved pine nuts. In a separate bowl, mix the tomato paste with the boiling water to make a thin sauce. Serve the quinoa on warm plates with the tomato sauce drizzled around the edge.

SLOW-COOKED GARLIC AND HERB PASTA

Preparation time: 2 minutes

Cooking time: 2½–3 hours

Serves **4**

Vegetarian

---

1 whole head garlic, unpeeled

100ml (3½fl oz) white wine, plus extra if needed

8–12 tbsp crème fraîche, or to taste

---

2 tbsp mixed chopped fresh herbs, such as mint, parsley and basil

---

Sea salt and freshly ground black pepper

400g (14oz) dried pasta, such as farfalle or fusilli

Slow cooking garlic makes it gloriously sweet in flavour and absolutely perfect in this creamy pasta dish. This is great with a tomato salad.

Place the whole garlic in the slow cooker dish and pour over the wine. Cover with the lid and cook on low for 2½–3 hours, adding more wine if it starts to boil dry, until the garlic is soft.

Remove the garlic from the slow cooker and, using a sharp knife, cut the top from the garlic to expose the tips of the cloves. Squeeze out the now softened flesh into a bowl and mash with a fork until smooth.

Add the crème fraîche and herbs together with any juices from the slow cooker and season to taste with salt and pepper. Mix well.

Cook the pasta in a large saucepan of salted boiling water according to the packet instructions or until tender but still firm to the bite (al dente).

Drain the pasta reasonably well leaving a little of the cooking water behind in the pan. Return the drained pasta to the pan, add the garlic sauce and mix to combine, then serve with a tomato salad.

I ALSO LIKE...

to roast another head or two of garlic at the same time and keeping them well wrapped in the fridge for up to two weeks. Try mixing some of the garlic into mayonnaise for sandwiches or to top jacket potatoes, or even blended with cream cheese and used as a dip for crudités or crisps.

BRAISED LENTIL SALAD

This simple, rustic salad is packed with flavour and is utterly more-ish. It's great on its own with crusty bread or equally at home as an accompaniment to meat, especially lamb.

Cover the base of the slow cooker dish with the olive oil. Using your thumb, press the garlic firmly to bruise it and add it to the slow cooker dish. Add the lentils, celery and herbs and mix well to coat in the oil.

Pour the stock over the lentils. Cover with the lid and cook on high for 3 hours or until the lentils are tender.

Remove from the heat and leave to cool completely. The mixture will be quite liquid. Season to taste with extra virgin olive oil and salt and pepper. Mix in the parsley before serving with lemon wedges.

Preparation time: 5 minutes
Cooking time: 3 hours
Serves 4 as a main salad
Vegetarian

4–6 tbsp olive oil

1 garlic clove, peeled

250g (9oz) Umbrian or brown lentils, rinsed and drained

1 celery stick, trimmed and finely diced

2 fresh thyme sprigs, leaves only

1 bay leaf, broken

A large pinch of dried basil

1 litre (1¾ pints) vegetable stock

Extra virgin olive oil, to taste

Sea salt and freshly ground black pepper

15g (½oz) fresh flat-leaf parsley, roughly chopped

Lemon wedges, to serve

RED PEPPER, BASIL AND RICOTTA CANNELLONI

Preparation time: 25 minutes
Cooking time: 2 hours 10 minutes
Serves 4

6 red peppers

250g (9oz) ricotta cheese

6–8 tbsp roughly chopped fresh basil

75g (3oz) finely grated fresh Parmesan cheese

Sea salt and freshly ground black pepper

12 dried cannelloni

200ml (7fl oz) milk

2 eggs

Basil leaves, to garnish

Basil makes this cannelloni amazingly fragrant while the ricotta filling helps keep the mixture light and refreshing.

Place the peppers under a preheated hot grill and cook for 10 minutes, turning frequently until completely blackened. Transfer to a large bowl, cover with cling film and leave to stand for 10 minutes. When cool, peel off the skin under cold running water, then remove and discard the seeds, stalk and any white membrane. Pat dry with kitchen paper.

Roughly chop the pepper flesh and place in a large mixing bowl. Add the ricotta, basil and one-third of the Parmesan cheese, season to taste with salt and pepper and mix well.

Remove the slow cooker dish from the base and preheat the slow cooker. Using a teaspoon or piping bag, fill the cannelloni with the ricotta mixture and arrange them in the slow cooker dish, in a single layer if possible.

Measure the milk into a jug. Add the eggs and whisk with a fork to combine. Add 25g (1oz) of the remaining Parmesan and mix in well. Season to taste and pour over the pasta. Cover with the lid and place the dish into the slow cooker base. Cook on high for 2 hours or until the pasta is tender. Five minutes before the end of cooking preheat the grill to its highest setting. If your slow cooker dish is flameproof (see manufacturer's instructions), sprinkle the remaining Parmesan over the top and place under the grill for 3–5 minutes or until golden. Serve immediately, garnished with basil leaves.

WILD MUSHROOM OPEN LASAGNE

A real treat when wild mushrooms are in season.

Butter the inside of the slow cooker dish. Place the mushrooms in the dish, add half of the butter, olive oil, 1 teaspoon of salt, the wine and garlic and mix well. Cover with the lid and cook on low for 4 hours or until softened.

About 30 minutes before you wish to eat, bring a large saucepan of salted water to the boil over a high heat. Place a clean tea towel onto a clean surface. Drop each lasagne sheet into the water for 1 minute or according to the packet instructions, then remove with a slotted spoon and place onto the prepared tea towel. Repeat with the other sheets, placing them in a single layer on the tea towel and interleaving them with more tea towels as required so that the lasagne sheets do not touch each other.

Place the crème fraîche and remaining butter in a small saucepan and warm over a medium heat until the butter has melted, then whisk the mixture until combined. Season the mushrooms and add the parsley.

Preheat the grill to its highest setting. Place a sheet of lasagne onto a warm deep serving plate. Top with a spoonful of the mushroom mixture and a drizzle of the crème fraîche sauce. Repeat three times finishing with the sauce. Sprinkle with Parmesan cheese and cook under the grill for 2–3 minutes or until golden. Keep warm while you repeat with the other plates.

Preparation time: 20 minutes
Cooking time: 4¼ hours
Serves 4

100g (3½oz) chilled butter, cubed, plus extra for greasing

750g (1lb 10oz) mixed wild mushrooms, such as morels, ceps and shiitake, wiped and cut into large wedges or thick slices

2 tbsp olive oil

Sea salt and freshly ground black pepper

3 tbsp dry white wine

1 garlic clove, peeled and crushed

16 sheets fresh or dried lasagne

200ml (7fl oz) crème fraiche

2 tbsp finely chopped fresh flat-leaf parsley

50g (2oz) freshly grated Parmesan cheese, plus extra to serve

SQUASH, SAGE AND WALNUT RISOTTO

Preparation time: 10 minutes
Cooking time: 2–3½ hours
Serves 4–6
Vegetarian

1 butternut squash, about 1kg
(2lb 4oz), peeled, deseeded and
cut into 2–3cm (¾–1¼in) cubes

4 large sage leaves, roughly
chopped, plus extra to serve

1 red onion, peeled, halved and thinly
sliced

2 garlic cloves, peeled and finely
chopped

2 tbsp olive oil

Sea salt and freshly ground black
pepper

350g (12oz) risotto rice, such as
Arborio

75ml (2½fl oz) marsala or sherry

1.3 litres (2¼ pints) vegetable stock,
plus extra to serve

50g (2oz) walnut pieces

Freshly grated Parmesan or
crumbled goat's cheese, to serve

This colourful risotto is made enticingly flavoursome by the slow-roasting of the squash, which concentrates its already sweet and fragrant flesh.

Place the squash, sage, onion and garlic in the slow cooker dish. Drizzle with the olive oil and season well with salt and pepper. Cover with the lid and cook on high for 1–2 hours, stirring once during cooking if you can, until tender and starting to colour slightly. Add the rice, marsala or sherry and stock and mix in gently being careful not to break up the squash. Reduce the heat to low, cover and cook for a further 1–1½ hours or until the rice is tender but still has a little bite (al dente).

Season to taste and add a splash of hot stock if you like your risotto creamy. Sprinkle with the walnuts and some extra sage. Serve topped with plenty of Parmesan or crumbled goat's cheese and a tomato, red onion and balsamic salad on the side.

I ALSO LIKE...

roasting a double batch of squash and keeping some in the freezer for another risotto. Alternatively, you can blitz the squash with stock to make a delicious soup, or toss through freshly cooked pasta with some mascarpone to make a great sauce.

GARLIC CHICKEN CARBONARA

Preparation time: 10 minutes
Cooking time: 2–3 hours
Serves 4

300g (10oz) boneless chicken breast, about 2 breasts, cut into 2cm (¾in) pieces

100g (3½oz) pancetta, cut into 2cm (¾in) pieces

1 tbsp plain flour

1 garlic clove, peeled and finely chopped

100ml (3½fl oz) white wine

Sea salt and freshly ground black pepper

100ml (3½fl oz) double cream

400g (14oz) dried spaghetti

2 egg yolks, beaten

2 tbsp chopped fresh flat-leaf parsley

This is a simple family favourite with the addition of slow-cooked chicken breast. It's great for informal entertaining too.

Place the chicken and pancetta in the slow cooker dish and sprinkle the flour over the top. Mix well with a wooden spoon until the meat is coated in the flour. Add the garlic and wine and season generously with salt and pepper. Cover with the lid and cook on low for 2–3 hours, stirring every now and again if you're around, until the sauce is thick and no longer tastes floury.

After cooking, remove the slow cooker dish from the heated base and beat in the cream, making sure there are no lumps remaining. Leave to stand for about 5 minutes to cool slightly.

Meanwhile, bring a large pan of salted water to the boil. Add the spaghetti and cook for 10 minutes or until tender but still firm to the bite (al dente). Drain, keeping about 2 tablespoons of the cooking water if you can.

Add the egg yolks to the chicken mixture and mix quickly to combine. Check the seasoning, adding more salt and pepper if necessary.

Tip the cooked pasta and the reserved cooking water into the sauce and mix well. Scatter the chopped parsley over the top and serve immediately on warm plates with a green salad.

ONE-POT MOROCCAN CHICKEN WITH COUSCOUS

This easy recipe tastes fabulous and is just as good for entertaining as it is for a mid-week supper.

Season the chicken legs with salt and pepper. Warm the olive oil and butter in a large frying pan. When hot, add the chicken legs and cook for about 5 minutes or until golden on both sides. Arrange the chicken in the slow cooker dish in a single layer and pour any cooking juices over the top. Scatter the diced onions in a layer over the chicken and add the garlic, spices and citrus zest.

Using a small, serrated knife, cut the top and bottom from the citrus fruit, then place them on a board and slice off the peel in downward strips, being careful to remove the pith as well. Holding the citrus fruit over a small bowl to catch any juice, slice between the thin membranes to release the segments. Do this with each orange and the lemon and add the segments to the chicken together with any juice. Cover with the lid and cook on low for 4-5 hours or until the chicken is tender and there is no pink meat.

Thirty minutes before you wish to eat, sprinkle the couscous over the top and cover again. Cook for 30 minutes or until the couscous is tender. Run a fork through the couscous to separate the grains, then spoon onto warm plates and top with the chicken and sauce. Sprinkle the coriander over and serve. Great with a dressed green salad.

Preparation time: 10 minutes
Cooking time: 4¼–5¼ hours
Serves 4

Sea salt and freshly ground black pepper

4 chicken legs, skin removed

1 tbsp olive oil

25g (1oz) butter

2 large onions, peeled and finely diced

2 garlic cloves, peeled and crushed

1 tsp ground cinnamon

1 tsp ground ginger

Finely grated zest of 2 oranges

Finely grated zest of 1 lemon (preferably unwaxed)

250g (9oz) couscous

4 tbsp roughly chopped fresh coriander leaves

ITALIAN SAUSAGE AND RED WINE RAGOUT

Preparation time: 10 minutes
Cooking time: 4¼–6¼ hours, plus cooking the pasta
Serves 4

400g (14oz) (about 6) fresh Italian sausages (most major supermarkets have an Italian variety in their sausage selection)

2 tbsp olive oil

1 tsp fennel seeds

1 red onion, peeled, halved and finely sliced

2 garlic cloves, peeled and crushed

1 x 400g (14oz) tin chopped tomatoes

2 tbsp concentrated tomato purée

1 bay leaf, broken

A small pinch of dried basil

100ml (3½fl oz) red wine

350g (12oz) dried pasta, such as tagliatelle or spaghetti

2 tbsp chopped fresh flat-leaf parsley

Sea salt and freshly ground black pepper

Parmesan cheese, to serve

This tasty dish is great for a mid-week supper, or served from a large platter when entertaining at home.

Squeeze the sausage meat out of the sausage skins and roll the contents of each one into 6–7 little balls.

Pour half of the olive oil into the slow cooker dish. Warm the remainder in a large frying pan over a high heat, and when hot add the fennel and cook for about 30 seconds or until fragrant. Add the sausage balls to the hot frying pan and cook until browned all over. Using a slotted spoon transfer the sausage balls to the slow cooker dish.

Add the onion to the slow cooker dish together with the garlic, tomatoes, tomato purée, bay leaf, basil and wine. Cover with the lid and cook on low for 4–6 hours. Don't be tempted to remove the lid during cooking.

When you are ready to eat, cook the pasta in a large saucepan of boiling, salted water according to the packet instructions or until firm to the bite (al dente). Drain the pasta, leaving a little of the cooking water (about 2 tablespoons) behind in the pan. Tip the pasta and reserved water into the sausage sauce and fold through together with the parsley. Season to taste with salt and pepper. Serve with a block of Parmesan cheese to grate over the top.

FAB FOR THE FREEZER
This sauce freezes really well and will keep for up to three months. Make sure you defrost it thoroughly before gently reheating on the hob (never in the slow cooker). Serve with freshly cooked pasta.

CREAMY PANCETTA AND BLUE CHEESE RISOTTO

Preparation time: 10 minutes
Cooking time: 1¾ hours
Serves 6

125g (4½oz) cubed pancetta

1 large onion, peeled and diced

400g (14oz) risotto rice, such as Arborio

2 garlic cloves, peeled and finely chopped

100ml (3½fl oz) dry white wine

1.3 litres (2¼ pints) hot chicken or vegetable stock, plus extra if needed

2 fresh thyme sprigs, plus extra to garnish

100g (3½oz) blue cheese, such as Italian dolcelatte

Sea salt and freshly ground black pepper

Rich and warming but not heavy, this risotto is just as good for a light summer lunch with salad as it is in the middle of winter with hot buttered vegetables.

Warm a large frying pan over a medium heat. When hot, add the pancetta and cook for about 30 seconds. Add the onion, reduce the heat and stir-fry for about 5 minutes or until the onion is softened but not coloured.

Increase the heat slightly, then add the rice and mix well until the rice is coated in the bacon fat. Stir in the garlic and wine and cook for a further minute or until the wine has been absorbed by the rice.

Spoon the mixture into the slow cooker dish and add the stock and thyme. Cover with the lid and cook on low for 1½ hours or until all the stock has been absorbed and the rice is tender but still has a little bite (al dente).

Add a splash of hot stock if you like your risotto creamy, then crumble the cheese over the risotto, season generously with salt and pepper and stir in roughly. Leave to stand for 2 minutes before serving with rocket leaves and a tomato and onion salad.

I ALSO LIKE...
to use a strong goat's cheese instead of the blue cheese.

EASY MUSHROOM AND PARMA HAM LASAGNE

This recipe is so easy to make and perfect for a family supper or relaxed entertaining.

Remove the slow cooker dish from the base and rub the butter generously over the inside of the dish. Turn the slow cooker base (without the dish in it) on to high to preheat.

Warm the olive oil in large frying pan over a high heat. When very hot, add the mushrooms and season generously with salt and pepper. Cook for 5 minutes, stirring occasionally, until the mushrooms are golden. Add the pasta sauce to the pan. Fill the jar a third full with cold water and rinse out the contents into the pan. Add the ham and mix well.

Spread about 4 tablespoons of the mushroom sauce over the base of the slow cooker dish. Top with 3 sheets of the lasagne, about a third of the remaining sauce and a third of the cheeses. Repeat this process twice more but do not cover with the final layer of cheese (the top layer should be the mushroom sauce). Insert the dish carefully into the preheated slow cooker base, cover with the lid and cook on low for 4–6 hours or until the pasta is tender when tested with the tip of a knife.

Once cooked, remove the lid and sprinkle over the reserved cheese. Leave uncovered for about 10–15 minutes or until the cheese has melted. Serve with a dressed green salad.

Preparation time: 5 minutes
Cooking time: 4½–6½ hours, plus preheating
Serves 6

A large knob of butter

2 tbsp olive oil

500g (1lb 2oz) sliced white mushrooms

Sea salt and freshly ground black pepper

700g (1lb 9oz) jar good-quality tomato pasta sauce

12 very thin slices of prosciutto di Parma (ham), shredded into 1–2cm (½–¾in) pieces

About 9 sheets white 'no need to pre-cook' dried lasagne

150g (5oz) grated mozzarella cheese

25g (1oz) freshly grated Parmesan cheese

SPICED LAMB PILAF

Preparation time: 15 minutes
Cooking time: 8½–9½ hours
Serves 4

½ tbsp olive oil

500g (1lb 2oz) lamb neck fillet, cut into 3cm (1¼in) pieces

2 red onions, peeled and finely sliced

½ tsp dried red chilli flakes

2 garlic cloves, peeled and crushed

50g (2oz) pine nuts

1 tsp ground coriander

½ tsp turmeric

1 tsp ground ginger

1 tsp ground cinnamon

400ml (14fl oz) white wine

Sea salt and freshly ground black pepper

200g (7oz) basmati rice

This Moroccan-inspired pilaf is fantastic – fragrant and spicy with plenty of different textures and tons of flavour. Most importantly, the slow cooking leaves the lamb neck irresistibly tender.

Warm half of the oil in a frying pan over a high heat. When hot, add the lamb and cook until browned on all sides. Spoon into the slow cooker dish.

Return the pan to the heat and add the remaining oil. Reduce the heat to medium and add the onions, chilli, garlic, pine nuts, coriander, turmeric, ginger and cinnamon and cook for about 5 minutes or until the spices are wonderfully aromatic and the onion is softened. Reduce the heat during cooking if the spices or pine nuts start to burn.

Add the wine to the pan and mix well. Bring to the boil, then pour this over the lamb. Season generously with salt and pepper. Cover with the lid and cook on low for 8–9 hours.

When you get back from work or 30 minutes before you want to eat, place the rice in a sieve. Pour a kettle full of freshly boiled water over the rice and drain. Fold the wet rice into the lamb mixture.

Cover with the lid again and cook for a further 30 minutes or until the rice is tender and has absorbed most of the cooking liquid. Season to taste.

PROPER BOLOGNESE

Preparation time: 10 minutes
Cooking time: 8¼–10¼ hours
Serves 6

2 tbsp olive oil

250g (9oz) pancetta or streaky bacon, cut into cubes

1kg (2lb 4oz) coarse ground beef mince

250ml (9fl oz) red wine

2 garlic cloves, peeled and roughly chopped

500g (1lb 2oz) onions, peeled and finely chopped

2 celery sticks, trimmed and diced

1 large carrot, peeled and diced

1 x 400g (14oz) tin chopped tomatoes

250ml (9fl oz) tomato passata

1 beef stock cube, crumbled

2 bay leaves, broken

Sea salt and freshly ground black pepper

Our friend Neil lived and worked in Italy for a while, and as a result makes the best bolognese ever! Here's my version, using some of his top tips, and a few of my own ideas, to make a slow cooker 'spag bol' that I hope he will love.

Warm the olive oil in a large frying pan over a high heat. When hot, add the pancetta or bacon and cook for 2–3 minutes or until it becomes opaque. Add the mince in batches and cook for 5–10 minutes or until browned, spooning the cooked batches into the slow cooker dish with a slotted spoon as it cooks.

Return the pan to the heat and add the wine. Cook for 1 minute, stirring constantly to scrape any tasty bits from the bottom of the pan. Pour into the slow cooker. Add the garlic, onions, celery, carrot, tomatoes, passata, stock cube and bay leaves to the mince and mix well. Cover with the lid and cook on low for 8–10 hours or until thick and rich.

Season with plenty of salt and pepper and serve with freshly cooked spaghetti. For me, a dressed green salad with plenty of cucumber is essential to go alongside, as well as lots of freshly grated Parmesan cheese and freshly ground black pepper.

FAB FOR THE FREEZER
This dish is always welcome in our house and can be reheated gently from frozen on the hob (never in the slow cooker). Make sure it's piping hot before serving with freshly cooked pasta.

VEAL RAGOUT

This rich, glossy ragout is packed with flavour and is incredibly easy to make. It makes a lighter alternative to beef mince.

Warm half of the olive oil in a large frying or sauté pan over a medium heat. When hot, add the vegetables and sauté gently, stirring occasionally, for 5 minutes or until softened but not coloured. Spoon into the slow cooker dish.

Return the pan to the heat and increase the temperature to high. When hot, add the remaining olive oil and warm through for a moment before adding the veal. Fry for 8–10 minutes, stirring very occasionally, or until the mince is well browned.

Add the mince to the slow cooker dish and stir in the flour. Add the wine, bay leaves and stock, cover with the lid and cook on low for 6–8 hours or until rich and thick.

Mix in the parsley and season to taste with salt and pepper. Spoon over freshly cooked pappardelle pasta to serve. Great with a dressed green salad.

FAB FOR THE FREEZER
Cook a double batch and freeze it in portions for those evenings when you don't have the energy or the inclination to cook.

Preparation time: 5 minutes
Cooking time: 6½–8½ hours
Serves 4

2 tbsp olive oil

1 large red onion, peeled and cut into 5mm (¼in) dice

2 celery sticks, (choose the darkest green stalks for flavour), trimmed and cut into 5mm (¼in) dice

450g (1lb) minced veal

1 tbsp plain flour

150ml (5fl oz) red wine

4 bay leaves, broken

500ml (18fl oz) hot vegetable stock

6 tbsp finely chopped fresh flat-leaf parsley

Sea salt and freshly ground black pepper

SPAGHETTI AND MEATBALLS

Preparation time: 15 minutes
Cooking time: 8¼ hours
Serves 4

1 large onion, peeled and finely diced

1 green pepper, deseeded and finely diced

1 garlic clove, peeled and crushed

2 x 400g (14oz) tins chopped tomatoes

2 tbsp tomato purée

1 tbsp soft dark brown sugar

1 tsp dried oregano

2 bay leaves

Sea salt and freshly ground black pepper

FOR THE MEATBALLS:

500g (1lb 2oz) lean beef mince

1 egg, slightly beaten

2 tbsp finely grated Parmesan cheese, plus extra to serve

½ tsp sea salt

A family classic made extra flavoursome and rich with long, slow cooking. This is great with a green salad.

Place the onion and diced pepper in the slow cooker dish together with the remaining sauce ingredients. Mix well and season with salt and pepper. Cover with the lid and cook on high while you prepare the meatballs.

Place the mince into a large mixing bowl and add the egg, Parmesan cheese and salt. Mix well with your hand for at least 2–3 minutes or until the mince is smooth and blended very thoroughly with the other ingredients.

Dampen your clean hands with cold water and roll the mince mixture into 16 even, walnut-sized balls. When they are all prepared drop them gently into the slow cooker dish. Using a wooden spoon or spatula, carefully fold the meatballs into the sauce, being careful not to break them up. Cover with the lid and reduce the temperature to low. Cook for 8 hours, without stirring, until the sauce has thickened and the meatballs are tender.

Stir gently to mix and season to taste. Discard the bay leaves and serve spooned over hot, freshly cooked spaghetti with plenty of grated Parmesan.

PARTY PAELLA FOR A CROWD

Preparation time: 20 minutes
Cooking time: 4½–5½ hours
Serves 10

2 tbsp olive oil

200g (7oz) chorizo, cut into chunks

4 garlic cloves, peeled and finely chopped

2 onions, peeled and finely diced

2 red peppers, deseeded and diced

1½ tsp fresh thyme leaves

½ tsp dried chilli flakes

1 tsp paprika

750g (1lb 10oz) long grain rice

200ml (7fl oz) dry white wine

1 litre (1¾ pints) chicken stock

A large pinch of saffron strands

150g (5oz) frozen petit pois

1 x 400g (14oz) tin chopped tomatoes, drained (keep the juice for cooking or for a Bloody Mary the morning after the party!)

10 chicken thighs, skinned

25g (1oz) butter

20 large raw shell-on prawns

30 small clams, cleaned (optional)

6 tbsp finely chopped fresh flat-leaf parsley

Sea salt and freshly ground black pepper

I love paella, but it can overcook without lots of careful watching. The slow cooker takes all the hassle out of it, giving you plenty of time to prepare and resulting in an easy, hot meal for a crowd a few hours later. Perfect! You will need a large 5–6 litre (9–10½ pint) slow cooker for this quantity, or adjust the amounts accordingly.

Warm half the olive oil in a large frying pan over a high heat. When hot, add the chorizo and cook for 5 minutes or until the orangey oils are released. Add three-quarters of the garlic, the onions and red peppers and continue cooking for a further 5 minutes or until soft. Mix in the thyme, chilli flakes and paprika, then spoon into the slow cooker dish with any cooking juices. Add the rice, wine, stock, saffron, peas, tomatoes and chicken and mix well. Cover with the lid and cook on low for 4–5 hours or until the liquid has been absorbed and the rice is tender.

Warm the remaining olive oil and the butter together in a large clean frying pan over a high heat. When hot, add the reserved garlic, followed by the prawns and clams (if using) and cook for 5–10 minutes, shaking the pan occasionally, until all the prawns are pink and the clams have opened. Discard any unopened clams.

Stir the parsley into the rice and season to taste. Distribute the hot shellfish over the top together with any pan juices, and serve immediately.

I ALSO LIKE...

to add rabbit pieces on the bone to this dish – add them instead of, or as well as, the chicken.

TOMATO AND ROCKET RISOTTO

This risotto is SO easy to make – there's no standing over a pot stirring for ages. Instead everything is mixed together and then left to its own devices.

Warm a quarter of the olive oil in a frying pan over a medium-low heat. When hot, add the onion and garlic and sweat gently without colouring for about 5 minutes.

Cover the base of the slow cooker dish with the remaining olive oil. Place the cooked onion and garlic into the dish together with the butter, rice, stock and tomatoes and mix well. Cover with the lid and cook on low for 2 hours or until the rice has absorbed the liquid. Don't be tempted to stir or remove the lid.

Stir in the Parmesan and season to taste with salt and pepper. Fold the rocket through the risotto and serve with plenty of Parmesan to sprinkle over.

COOKING CONVENTIONALLY?
Follow the recipe using a large casserole dish with a tight-fitting lid instead of the slow cooker dish. Add 250ml (9fl oz) cold water before cooking in an oven preheated to 180°C (350°F), Gas mark 4, for 1 hour or until tender, then stir in the rocket and Parmesan and serve.

Preparation time: 5 minutes
Cooking time: 2 hours 10 minutes
Serves 4

4 tbsp good-quality olive oil

1 onion, peeled and finely diced

1 garlic clove, peeled and crushed

25g (1oz) butter

250g (9oz) risotto rice

750ml (1¼ pints) chicken or vegetable stock

1 x 400g (14oz) tin chopped tomatoes

25g (1oz) freshly grated Parmesan cheese, plus extra to serve

Sea salt and freshly ground black pepper

2 handfuls of rocket leaves

EASY BEEF RAGOUT

Preparation time: 10 minutes
Cooking time: 6–8 hours
Serves 8

1 large onion, peeled and diced

2 large carrots, peeled and diced

2 celery sticks, trimmed and cut into 1cm (½in) pieces

3 garlic cloves, peeled and roughly chopped

550g (1lb 4oz) extra lean, 5% fat beef mince

2 beef stock cubes

250ml (9fl oz) red wine

2 tbsp concentrated tomato purée

1 tsp good-quality dried oregano

4 x 400g (14oz) tins chopped tomatoes

Sea salt and freshly ground black pepper

About 2 tbsp caster sugar, or to taste

Freshly grated Parmesan cheese, for sprinkling

Beef mince should almost always be full fat – the fat giving it a wonderful flavour and texture. However, there are times when extra lean mince is perfect, and this recipe is one of them. Use good-quality extra lean beef mince with about 5% fat, add lots of vegetables and it's as easy as that.

Place the vegetables and garlic into the slow cooker dish. Crumble the mince and the stock cube over the vegetables, add the red wine, tomato purée, oregano and tomatoes and mix well, using the spoon to break up any large lumps of mince.

Cover with the lid and cook on high for 6–8 hours, stirring occasionally if you are around, until reduced and the tomato has cooked down. Season generously with salt and pepper, and the sugar to taste.

Serve on a bed of freshly cooked spaghetti with plenty of Parmesan cheese sprinkled over, and a green salad on the side.

I ALSO LIKE...
to add some dried chilli flakes at the beginning and a tin of drained red kidney beans 30 minutes before the end of cooking for an easy chilli to serve with rice.

CHILLIES, CURRIES
+
SPICY FOOD

CHICKPEA AND SWEET POTATO CHILLI

Preparation time: 10 minutes
Cooking time: 4–5 hours
Serves 4
Vegetarian

2 tbsp olive oil

1 large red chilli, deseeded and finely chopped

1 garlic clove, peeled and finely chopped

2.5cm (1in) piece fresh root ginger, peeled and finely chopped

1 large red onion, peeled and cut into 2cm (¾in) pieces

2 red peppers, deseeded and cut into 2cm (¾in) pieces

½ tsp ground cumin

2 sweet potatoes, about 350g (12oz) each, peeled and cut into 2cm (¾in) pieces

1 x 410g tin chickpeas, rinsed and drained

2 tbsp orange juice

2 tbsp soured cream, plus extra to serve

Sea salt and freshly ground black pepper

4 tbsp chopped fresh coriander

This colourful vegetarian chilli looks and tastes fantastic. If you like your food spicy, leave the chilli seeds in.

Warm the olive oil in a large frying pan over a medium heat. When hot, add the chilli, garlic and ginger and cook for 30 seconds or until softened but not coloured. Add the onion, peppers and cumin and cook, stirring frequently, until softened but not coloured. Tip the mixture into the slow cooker dish, add the sweet potatoes, chickpeas and orange juice and stir well. Cover with the lid and cook on low for 4–5 hours or until the potato is tender.

Before serving, gently stir in the soured cream and season to taste with salt and pepper, being careful not to squish the sweet potatoes. Sprinkle over the coriander and serve with extra soured cream and flour tortillas.

COOKING CONVENTIONALLY?
Cook in an ovenproof casserole dish with a tight-fitting lid for 3 hours in an oven preheated to 150°C (300°F), Gas mark 2.

FOUR BEAN CHILLI

Preparation time: 5 minutes
Cooking time: 6¼ hours
Serves 6–8
Vegetarian

1 x 400g (14oz) tin butter beans

1 x 400g (14oz) tin red kidney beans

1 x 400g (14oz) tin black eye beans

1 x 400g (14oz) tin cannellini beans

25g (1oz) butter

2 tbsp olive oil

1 large onion, peeled and diced

2 garlic cloves, peeled and finely sliced

3 mixed colour peppers, deseeded and diced

1 x 400g (14oz) tin chopped tomatoes

1 tsp chilli powder, or to taste

2 tsp ground cumin

1 tsp ground coriander

1 tsp dried oregano

350ml (12fl oz) vegetable stock (try to use a low salt variety as salt will toughen the skins of the beans)

2 tbsp soured cream, plus extra to serve

Sea salt and freshly ground black pepper

This vegetarian chilli uses tinned beans so it is really easy to make. Vary the beans depending on what you prefer, and always have a few tins in the cupboard.

Place all the beans in a large sieve or colander and rinse under cold running water. Drain well.

Warm a large frying pan over a high heat. When hot, add the butter and olive oil. Once the butter has melted, add the onion and cook, stirring continuously, for 5 minutes or until it starts to soften. Add the garlic and peppers and cook for a further 5 minutes, stirring occasionally until they are softened and starting to colour. Reduce the heat if the vegetables are becoming any more than golden.

Add the vegetables to the slow cooker dish with the drained beans, the tomatoes, spices, oregano and stock. Cover with the lid and cook on low for 6 hours or until thickened.

Stir in the soured cream and season to taste with salt and pepper. Serve with freshly cooked rice and a dollop of soured cream.

THAI PUMPKIN SOUP

Butternut squash or pumpkin tastes great in Thai recipes. Here it makes a comforting, smooth soup, which is great for everyday food or as a starter when entertaining.

Place the butternut squash or pumpkin in the slow cooker dish together with the onion, ginger and curry paste and mix well until the pumpkin is coated. Cover with the lid and cook on high for 2 hours or until the squash is really tender. Remove the slow cooker dish from the base, but leave the slow cooker switched on.

Place the squash or pumpkin and any cooking juices into a food processor and blitz, adding a little of the hot stock to loosen the mixture, until smooth. Gradually add the remaining stock.

Return the mixture to the slow cooker dish and add the coconut milk, lime juice and fish sauce. Place the dish back onto the heated base and replace the lid. Cook for 1 hour or until hot.

Season the soup with more fish sauce and the sugar to taste. Ladle into warm bowls and sprinkle with coriander leaves before serving.

I ALSO LIKE...

cooking this recipe to the end of paragraph 1 and then mixing the squash or pumpkin cubes with all the other ingredients except the stock. It's great heated through and served with rice noodles.

Preparation time: 10 minutes

Cooking time: 3 hours

Serves 4–6

1.5kg (3lb 5oz) butternut squash or pumpkin, peeled, deseeded and cut into chunks

1 red onion, peeled and diced

2.5cm (1in) piece fresh root ginger, peeled and grated

1–2 tsp red Thai curry paste, or to taste

1 litre (1¾ pints) hot vegetable stock

150ml (5fl oz) coconut milk

1 tbsp lime juice

1 tbsp fish sauce, or to taste

1 tbsp demerara sugar

Fresh coriander leaves, to garnish

CAULIFLOWER AND PARSNIP ROYAL KORMA

Preparation time: 5 minutes
Cooking time: 2 hours
Serves 4
Vegetarian

1 large onion, peeled and diced

2 tbsp korma curry paste

400ml (14fl oz) can coconut milk (preferably organic)

50g (2oz) ground almonds

1 large parsnip, about 300g (10oz), peeled, cored and diced into 3cm (1¼in) chunks

1 medium cauliflower, cut into small florets

Fresh coriander leaves, to garnish

This is a wonderfully rich and flavoursome vegetarian korma, which becomes 'royal' with the addition of coconut milk in place of yogurt.

Place the onion in the slow cooker dish, add the curry paste and coconut milk and mix well. Gradually mix in the almonds, then stir in the parsnip and cauliflower.

Cover with the lid and cook on high for 2 hours or until the vegetables are tender.

Tear the coriander into rough pieces and sprinkle over the curry before serving with warm naan bread.

TRY...
This curry is even better when made 24 hours in advance. Keep covered in the fridge, then reheat thoroughly in a saucepan before serving.

SRI LANKAN VEGETABLE CURRY

Preparation time: 10 minutes, plus soaking

Cooking time: 3–4 hours

Serves 4

Vegetarian

1 tbsp black mustard seeds

250ml (9fl oz) hot vegetable stock

2 tbsp vegetable oil

2 green chillies

2.5cm (1in) piece fresh root ginger, peeled and chopped

1 tsp cumin seeds

½ tsp black onion seeds

¼ tsp fennel seeds

½ tsp turmeric

2 tsp ground coriander

1 onion, peeled and chopped

½ butternut squash, peeled and cut into cubes

200g (7oz) green beans, trimmed and halved

2 large carrots, peeled and cut into cubes

1 red pepper, deseeded and cut into cubes

½ medium cauliflower, cut into florets

200g (7oz) packet coconut cream

¼ tsp sea salt, plus extra to taste

1–2 tbsp muscovado sugar, or to taste

Roughly chopped coriander leaves, for sprinkling

Lime wedges, to serve

Here's my Anglo-Sri Lankan veggie curry in honour of my lovely friend Gayathri.

Place the mustard seeds in a small bowl and cover with half of the hot stock. Leave to soak for 30 minutes.

Warm the vegetable oil in a large frying pan over a high heat. When hot, add the chillies, ginger, cumin, black onion seeds and fennel seeds and cook, stirring constantly, for 2 minutes or until fragrant. Stir in the turmeric and coriander. Place the warmed spices in a blender or mortar together with the mustard seeds and soaking liquid and blitz or pound until smooth.

Spoon into the slow cooker dish together with the prepared vegetables, coconut cream and salt and mix well, adding the remaining stock as you do so. Cover with the lid and cook on low for 3–4 hours or until the vegetables are tender.

Season with the sugar and more salt to taste. Sprinkle over the chopped coriander and serve with lime wedges to squeeze over and plenty of rice.

TOMATO, POTATO AND COCONUT CURRY

This easy vegetarian curry is also great as a side dish, if you prefer.

Place the potatoes in a bowl and cover with cold water.

Warm a frying pan over a medium heat. When hot, add the vegetable oil, garlic, chilli and cumin seeds. Cook for 1–2 minutes, stirring until softened but not coloured.

Drain the potatoes and place them and the contents of the frying pan into the slow cooker dish. Add the turmeric, ground cumin, tomatoes, tomato purée, salt, coconut cream and water and mix well. Prod all the potatoes in so that they are covered by liquid (this will prevent them from turning brown). Cover with the lid and cook for 3 hours on low or until the potatoes are tender and the sauce has thickened.

Season with the sugar, vinegar and more salt to taste and sprinkle over the coriander leaves. Serve with naan bread.

I ALSO LIKE...
to add some chicken breast on the bone with the potatoes for a meaty version.

Preparation time: 15 minutes
Cooking time: 3 hours
Serves **6**
Vegetarian

5 medium potatoes, peeled and cut into 2cm (¾in) cubes

1 tbsp vegetable oil

6 garlic cloves, peeled and finely chopped

1 red chilli, finely diced (deseed if you like a milder curry)

1 tsp cumin seeds

½ tsp turmeric

2 tsp ground cumin

1 x 400g (14oz) tin chopped tomatoes

2 tbsp concentrated tomato purée

1 tsp sea salt

200ml (7fl oz) packet coconut cream

250ml (9fl oz) water

2 tsp caster sugar, or to taste

1 tsp red wine vinegar, or to taste

Fresh coriander leaves, for sprinkling

BEETROOT AND CUMIN CURRY

Preparation time: 10 minutes
Cooking time: 3–4 hours
Serves 6 as a side dish
Vegetarian

800g (1lb 12oz) fresh raw beetroot, peeled and cut into 2cm (¾in) cubes

2 tbsp vegetable oil

3 garlic cloves, peeled and crushed

1 tsp cumin seeds

1 tsp fennel seeds

½ tsp dried chilli flakes

½ tsp ground coriander

1 tsp turmeric

1 x 400g (14oz) tin chopped tomatoes

1 tbsp concentrated tomato purée

1 tsp sea salt

2 tbsp finely chopped fresh coriander

This easy vegetarian 'curry' is more of a vegetable side dish really, but it looks and tastes great and will stand up on its own as a main course when served with rice.

Place the beetroot in the slow cooker dish.

Warm the vegetable oil in a large frying pan. When hot, add the garlic, cumin, fennel and chilli flakes and stir for 30 seconds, then add the ground coriander and turmeric. Remove from the heat and spoon into the slow cooker dish. Stir in the tomatoes, tomato purée and salt. Cover with the lid and cook on low for 3–4 hours or until the beetroot is tender and the sauce has thickened.

Sprinkle over the chopped coriander and serve.

I ALSO LIKE…
to stir a little coconut cream into this curry when it has cooked, as a variation.

GREEN CHILLI DHAL

This recipe is really easy and cheap to make; it also freezes brilliantly so you can make extra and then freeze it in portions for your next curry. This dhal is great as a side dish or hearty enough to have on its own.

Warm the vegetable oil in a large frying pan over a medium heat. When hot, add the onion and cook for 5 minutes or until softened but not coloured. Mix in the garlic, ginger, chilli, salt and cumin and cook for a further 5 minutes, stirring frequently, until fragrant.

Spoon the contents of the pan into the slow cooker dish together with the lentils and stock and mix well. Cover with the lid and cook on low for 4–6 hours or until thickened and the lentils are tender and beginning to break down.

Season to taste with lime juice, half of the coriander leaves and some extra salt if needed. Sprinkle over the rest of the coriander leaves and serve with naan bread.

I ALSO LIKE...
to make a more substantial curry by adding chicken or lamb with the lentils.

Preparation time: 5 minutes
Cooking time: 4¼–6¼ hours
Serves 4
Vegetarian

1 tbsp vegetable oil

1 onion, peeled and finely diced

2 garlic cloves, peeled and finely chopped

2.5cm (1in) piece fresh root ginger, peeled and grated

1 large green chilli, finely chopped

½ tsp sea salt, plus extra to taste

1 tsp ground cumin

250g (9oz) red lentils, rinsed and drained

500ml (18fl oz) vegetable stock

1–2 tbsp lime juice, or to taste

A small handful of fresh coriander leaves

RED LENTIL AND TOMATO DHAL

This tastes great and is perfect as a side dish to go with curry or on its own with naan bread.

Add the onion and garlic to the slow cooker dish. Mix in all the remaining ingredients and season well with salt.

Cover with the lid and cook on low for 6 hours or until thickened and the lentils are tender and beginning to break down.

Serve topped with spoonfuls of natural yogurt or raita with poppadums or naan bread.

Preparation time: 5 minutes
Cooking time: 6 hours
Serves 4
Vegetarian

1 red onion, peeled and finely sliced

1 garlic clove, peeled and finely chopped

2 tbsp medium curry paste (choose a milder or hotter one if you prefer)

2 x 400g (14oz) tins chopped tomatoes

250g (9oz) red lentils, rinsed and drained

500ml (18fl oz) vegetable stock

Sea salt

PRAWN AND PUMPKIN CURRY

Preparation time: 10 minutes
Cooking time: 2–3 hours
Serves 4

---

1 orange-fleshed pumpkin or butternut squash, about 1kg (2lb 4oz), peeled, deseeded and cut into 2–3cm (¾–1¼in) chunks

---

3–4 tsp Thai red curry paste (see page 93 or use ready-made)

Juice of 1 lime

---

1 tbsp demerara sugar

200ml (7fl oz) tinned coconut milk

---

4 large handfuls of baby spinach leaves, washed

250g (9oz) raw tiger prawns

---

2 tbsp Thai fish sauce, or to taste

---

4 spring onions, including their green tops, trimmed and finely sliced

---

Fresh coriander leaves, to garnish

Lime wedges, to serve

Fresh, aromatic and colourful, this curry is easy to make and tastes wonderful.

Place the pumpkin in the slow cooker dish together with the Thai paste, lime juice and sugar and mix well. Cover with the lid and cook on high for 2–3 hours, stirring once during cooking if you can, until tender and beginning to caramelise.

Add the coconut milk, spinach and prawns. Cover again and cook for a further 15 minutes or until the prawns are pink and opaque.

Season with the fish sauce to taste, then ladle into warm bowls and scatter over the spring onions and coriander leaves. Serve with lime wedges to squeeze over and freshly cooked jasmine rice.

I ALSO LIKE...

to make a laksa-style soup. Add 200ml (7fl oz) hot vegetable stock and some cooked fine rice noodles with the fish sauce.

SPICY MIDDLE EASTERN FISH STEW

Preparation time: 10 minutes
Cooking time: 4–5 hours
Serves 4–6

1 red onion, peeled and cut into 1cm (½in) pieces

1 green pepper, deseeded and cut into 1cm (½in) pieces

2 tbsp olive oil, plus extra for oiling

1 garlic clove, peeled and finely sliced

1 x 400g (14oz) tin chopped tomatoes

A pinch of saffron strands (optional)

2–3 tsp harissa paste, or to taste

A large pinch of dried oregano

100ml (3½fl oz) dry white wine

1kg (2lb 4oz) firm white skinned fish fillets, such as haddock or pollack, cut into 4cm (1½in) chunks

500g (1lb 2oz) red snapper fillets, skin on and cut into 4cm (1½in) chunks

4 tbsp finely chopped fresh flat-leaf parsley

Sea salt and freshly ground black pepper

This aromatic stew is quick to prepare and then the slow cooker does the rest.

Place the vegetables in the slow cooker dish. Add the olive oil, garlic, tomatoes, saffron (if using), harissa, oregano and wine and mix well. Arrange the fish on top in an even layer. Press a piece of lightly oiled parchment paper onto the fish and push down on it gently (this will stop it from drying out). Cover with the lid and cook on low for 4–5 hours or until the fish is opaque.

Spoon the fish onto warm plates. Mix the parsley into the sauce and season to taste with salt and pepper. Spoon over the fish and serve with freshly cooked rice or couscous.

I ALSO LIKE...
to swap the fish for chicken in this recipe. Cook on low for 4–6 hours or until there is no pink meat.

MEXICAN CHICKEN MOLE WITH CHOCOLATE

This gorgeous recipe uses chipotle paste – a smoked chilli paste pronounced 'chip-oat-lay'. Most supermarkets or delicatessens sell it these days. The dark chocolate gives the sauce a glorious richness.

Warm the olive oil in a frying pan over a medium heat. When hot, add the chilli and cumin and stir-fry for 1 minute or until fragrant. Add the onion and garlic and cook for about 4 minutes or until the onion is lightly browned. Remove from the heat and stir in the almonds so that they absorb all the spicy oil.

Spoon the warm onion mixture into a food processor. Add the chipotle, sugar, salt, cinnamon, chocolate, vinegar, tomato purée and about half of the stock and blitz it to make a smooth, thick paste.

Spoon the spice paste into the slow cooker dish and add the chicken. Turn the chicken over in the paste to coat completely, then arrange the chicken in a single layer, skin side down, and pour over the remaining stock.

Cover with the lid and cook on low for 6–8 hours or until the chicken is meltingly tender and beginning to caramelise on the base of the dish. Serve with fresh coriander, and dollops of soured cream on the side.

Preparation time: 15 minutes
Cooking time: 6–8 hours
Serves 4

2 tbsp olive oil

½ tsp dried chilli flakes

½ tsp cumin seeds

1 red onion, peeled and diced

2 garlic cloves, peeled and roughly chopped

100g (3½oz) ground almonds

1 tsp chipotle (smoked chilli) paste

1 tbsp soft dark brown sugar

¼ tsp sea salt

¼ tsp ground cinnamon

25g (1oz) dark plain chocolate

1 tbsp red wine vinegar

2 tbsp tomato purée

250ml (9fl oz) hot chicken or vegetable stock

4 chicken legs

Fresh coriander leaves, to serve

SEA BASS WITH GREEN CHILLI AND CORIANDER

Preparation time: 15 minutes
Cooking time: 2–3 hours
Serves 2

1 large sea bass, about 600–800g (1lb 5oz–1lb 12oz) or to fit in your slow cooker dish without bending, cleaned and gutted

2.5cm (1in) piece fresh root ginger, peeled and roughly chopped

5 garlic cloves, peeled and roughly chopped

1 lemongrass stalk, trimmed and roughly chopped

2 tbsp vegetable oil, plus extra for oiling

1 large green chilli, deseeded and finely chopped

25g (1oz) fresh coriander sprigs, roughly chopped

2 tbsp lime juice

½ tsp sea salt

4 tbsp cold water, plus a little extra if necessary

Lime wedges, to garnish

Fresh coriander, to garnish

I love the sweet, salty, sour combination of flavours in this Southeast Asian dish.

Place a large piece of parchment paper in the slow cooker dish, pushing it down into the edges, but ensuring that there is plenty of paper hanging over the sides. Wash the fish under cold running water and pat dry with kitchen paper.

Place the ginger, garlic, lemongrass, vegetable oil, chilli, coriander, lime juice, salt and 2 tablespoons of the water into a food processor or mortar and blitz to make a smooth paste, adding a little more water if the paste is very thick.

Spread a little of the green paste over the parchment base in the slow cooker dish and drizzle over the remaining 2 tablespoons of water. Smother the fish inside and out with the rest of the green paste and place it into the dish. Fold the overhanging parchment over the fish and press down around the edges to make a spacious layer around the fish. Cover with the lid and cook on low for 2–3 hours or until the fish is tender and cooked through.

Unwrap the parchment ends and use these as handles to carefully lift the fish out of the slow cooker dish. Place on a warm platter, garnish with lime wedges and a few sprigs of coriander, and serve with freshly cooked plain rice.

MEXICAN MOLE

Preparation time: 15 minutes
Cooking time: 6¼–8¼ hours
Serves 6

800g (1lb 12oz) turkey mince

1 tbsp olive oil

1 onion, peeled and diced

2 carrots, peeled and diced

2 celery sticks, trimmed and diced

2 bay leaves, broken

2 tbsp concentrated tomato purée

2 tbsp red wine vinegar

1 tsp muscovado sugar, plus extra to taste

250ml (9fl oz) chicken stock

50g (2oz) good-quality plain dark chocolate (at least 70% cocoa solids)

Sea salt and freshly ground black pepper

FOR THE SPICE PASTE:

3 red chillies, deseeded and chopped

75g (3oz) sesame seeds

50g (2oz) whole blanched almonds

50g (2oz) natural peanuts

50g (2oz) raisins

1 tsp coriander seeds

¼ tsp ground cinnamon

12 black peppercorns

6 whole cloves

4 garlic cloves, peeled and roughly chopped

2 tbsp cold water

Turkey mole is a much-loved Mexican feast day dish.

Pat the mince dry with kitchen paper. Warm the olive oil in a large frying pan over a high heat. When hot, add the mince and cook for 5–10 minutes, stirring continuously until well browned. Add the mince to the slow cooker dish together with the onion, carrots, celery, bay leaves, tomato purée, vinegar, sugar and stock, and mix well.

Return the pan to the heat to make the paste. When hot, add the chillies, seeds and nuts and cook for 2–3 minutes or until golden but not browned. Add half the raisins, coriander seeds, cinnamon, peppercorns, cloves and garlic and cook for a further minute or until fragrant. Tip the contents of the frying pan into a food processor and blitz with the water to make a thick paste. Alternatively, use a pestle and mortar.

Mix the paste and the remaining whole raisins with the turkey in the slow cooker dish. Cover with the lid and cook for 6–8 hours or until thick.

Grate the chocolate over the mince mixture and leave to melt in. Stir well and season with more sugar, salt and pepper. Serve with soft flour tortillas and soured cream.

THAI CHICKEN WITH HOME-MADE CURRY PASTE

If you don't have time to create your own curry paste, use a good-quality shop-bought paste instead and use about 2–3 tablespoonfuls. Buy fresh kaffir lime leaves from Asian food stores or freeze-dried from some major supermarkets.

Place all the curry paste ingredients in a food processor and blitz to make a textured mixture. Spoon the paste into the slow cooker dish and gradually mix in the coconut milk.

Place the vegetables in the slow cooker dish, then add the chicken and mix well to ensure it is immersed in the coconut milk.

Cover with the lid and cook on low for 6–9 hours or until the chicken is tender and the coconut milk has reduced slightly. If the sauce looks as if it has split, don't worry, just give it a good stir. Season with the sugar, fish sauce and lime juice to taste and serve with lime wedges on the side.

Preparation time: 15 minutes
Cooking time: 6–9 hours
Serves **4**

1 x 400ml (14fl oz) tin coconut milk

1 red pepper, deseeded and cut into strips

125g (4½oz) green beans, trimmed and cut into 4cm (1½in) lengths

125g (4½oz) aubergine, trimmed and cut into 2cm (¾in) cubes

4 boneless, skinless chicken breasts

½ tbsp caster sugar, or to taste

Thai fish sauce, to taste

Lime juice, to taste

Lime wedges, to serve

FOR THE CURRY PASTE:

2 shallots, peeled and chopped

1 lemongrass stalk, peeled and roughly chopped

2 tsp chopped fresh root ginger

1 tsp shredded fresh kaffir lime leaves

2 red bird's eye chillies, deseeded if you like

3 garlic cloves, peeled

½ tsp coriander seeds

½ tsp cumin seeds

2 tbsp Thai fish sauce

A large pinch of turmeric

CHILLI-CHICKEN TORTILLAS

Preparation time: 5 minutes
Cooking time: 6–8 hours
Serves 4

8 chicken thighs on the bone, skin removed

2 garlic cloves, peeled and thinly sliced

125g (4½oz) good-quality bought (fresh or from a jar) mild tomato salsa, plus extra to serve

1 large green chilli, finely chopped

1 tsp smoked paprika

½ tsp ground cumin

Sea salt and freshly ground black pepper

1 tbsp fresh coriander leaves

4 large flour tortillas or wraps, to serve

This simple recipe is great during the week and couldn't be easier to assemble. The tasty chicken is fabulous in tortillas or equally good in tacos or as a topping for nachos.

Place the chicken thighs, garlic, salsa, chilli, paprika and cumin in the slow cooker dish and season generously with salt and pepper. Cover with the lid and cook on low for 6–8 hours or until the chicken is tender and there is no pink meat.

Remove the chicken from the slow cooker dish and place on a plate or board. Use 2 forks to shred the meat and discard the bones. Moisten the meat with some of the cooking juices. Add the coriander, then taste and add more seasoning if necessary.

To serve, fold a tortilla in half and then in half again. Open the quartered tortilla to make a pocket. Pile the meat into the pocket and top with more salsa. Serve with some grated Cheddar cheese, shredded lettuce and soured cream or your own choice of toppings.

I ALSO LIKE...
tossing this chicken mixture through freshly cooked pasta – not really geographically correct, but it tastes great!

EASY CHICKEN KORMA

Preparation time: 20 minutes, plus marinating (optional)
Cooking time: 6 hours
Serves 4

8 chicken thighs on the bone, skin removed

400g (14oz) full-fat Greek yogurt

6 tbsp good-quality korma curry paste, or to taste

6 tbsp good-quality mango chutney

1 onion, peeled, halved and thinly sliced

1 red pepper, deseeded and diced

2 large ripe tomatoes, roughly chopped

2 tbsp water

100g (3½oz) baby spinach leaves

Sea salt and freshly ground black pepper

A handful of fresh coriander leaves

Chicken korma has become a family favourite. Here is a very easy version, perfect for a mid-week meal. If you prefer your curry to be hotter then use a stronger curry paste or simply use more of the korma paste!

Rinse the chicken thighs under cold running water, remove the skin and pat dry with kitchen paper.

Mix the yogurt, curry paste and mango chutney together in the slow cooker dish. Add the chicken and turn until the chicken is coated. If you have time, cover and place in the fridge for 30–60 minutes to marinate.

Mix the onion, pepper and tomatoes in with the chicken and drizzle over the water. Cover with the lid and cook on low for 6 hours or until the chicken is tender and there is no more pink meat.

Carefully remove the chicken from the slow cooker and place on warm plates or bowls. Add the spinach to the slow cooker dish and mix in until wilted. Season to taste with salt and pepper and sprinkle the coriander leaves over the top. Serve with rice, poppadums and chutneys.

I ALSO LIKE...
to make this with chicken legs or breast on the bone – without the bones the chicken will dry out very quickly.

TANDOOR-STYLE CHICKEN

If you use a good-quality tandoori paste for this recipe there's no need to make your own.

Using a sharp knife, slash each chicken thigh three times down to the bone and place in a shallow dish.

Mix the remaining ingredients together in a bowl and spoon over the chicken. Mix well until the chicken is coated in the yogurt mixture. Cover and chill for at least 3 hours or overnight.

The next morning or when you are ready to cook, preheat the slow cooker on high for 30 minutes. Arrange the chicken skin side down in a single layer in the warmed slow cooker dish. Cover with the lid and cook for 3–4 hours or until the chicken is tender and browned. Serve with warm naan bread and salad.

I ALSO LIKE...
coating a whole chicken or baby poussin with the spicy yogurt mixture and cooking in the slow cooker until tender and the juices run clear when the thickest part of the meat is pierced with a skewer.

Preparation time: **10 minutes, plus 3 hours marinating**
Cooking time: **3–4 hours**
Serves **4**

8 chicken thighs

125g (4½oz) natural yogurt

3–4 tbsp tandoori paste, to taste

1 garlic clove, peeled and crushed

1 tbsp lime juice

2 tbsp finely chopped fresh mint

PORK AND BORLOTTI BEAN CHILLI

Preparation time: 10 minutes
Cooking time: 6½–8½ hours
Serves 6

500g (1lb 2oz) pork shoulder or mince

1 large red onion, peeled and cut into 5mm–1cm (¼–½in) cubes

2 red peppers, deseeded and cut into 5mm–1cm (¼–½in) cubes

2 garlic cloves, peeled and crushed

1–2 tsp of chipotle (smoked chilli) paste or 1 large red chilli, deseeded and finely chopped

1½ tsp ground cumin

1 tbsp concentrated tomato purée

Juice of 1 large orange

150ml (5fl oz) hot chicken or pork stock

2 x 400g (14oz) tins borlotti beans, rinsed and drained

4 tbsp finely chopped fresh coriander

Sea salt and freshly ground black pepper

This is a great alternative chilli recipe. Chipotle paste (smoked chilli paste) is available at most good supermarkets and delicatessens.

If you're using pork shoulder cut the meat into small pieces about 5mm–1cm (¼–½in) in size. Place the shoulder or mince into the slow cooker dish together with the onion and peppers. Add the garlic, chipotle paste or chilli, cumin, tomato purée, orange juice and stock and mix well. Cover with the lid and cook on low for 6–8 hours.

Stir in the borlotti beans, cover again and cook on high for a further 30 minutes or until piping hot.

Stir in the coriander and season to taste with salt and pepper. Serve immediately with freshly cooked rice or flour tortillas and soured cream.

COOKING CONVENTIONALLY?
Preheat the oven to 150°C (300°F), Gas mark 2, and cook in an ovenproof casserole dish with a tight-fitting lid with an extra 200ml (7fl oz) cold water for 3 hours or until tender.

INDONESIAN PORK

Kecap manis is a dark, thick, sweet soy sauce and is available from Asian supermarkets.

Rinse the pork under cold running water and pat dry with kitchen paper. Cut the meat into 3–4cm (1¼–1½in) cubes and place in the slow cooker dish together with the tomatoes and pepper.

Place all the paste ingredients in a food processor and blend to make a smooth paste, adding a dash of cold water to loosen it. Mix the paste with the meat, add the remaining desiccated coconut and the sugar and mix until everything is evenly coated.

Cover with the lid and cook on low for 6–8 hours or until the meat is wonderfully tender. Season with a little fish sauce and lime juice to taste, and serve with lime wedges to squeeze over just before eating.

FAB FOR THE FREEZER
This recipe freezes really well for up to three months. Make sure you defrost it thoroughly before gently reheating on the hob (never in the slow cooker).

Preparation time: 20 minutes
Cooking time: 6–8 hours
Serves 6

850g (1lb 14oz) pork shoulder or leg

4 tomatoes, cut into 1cm (½in) pieces

1 red pepper, deseeded and cut into 1cm (½in) pieces

25g (1oz) desiccated coconut

1 tbsp demerara sugar

Fish sauce, or to taste

Lime juice, or to taste

Lime wedges, to serve

FOR THE PASTE:

1 red chilli, (deseeded if you prefer a milder curry)

1 small onion, peeled and cut into chunks

4 garlic cloves, peeled

1 lemongrass stalk, trimmed and roughly chopped

About 5cm (2in) piece fresh root ginger

1 tbsp dark soy sauce or kecap manis

75g (3oz) desiccated coconut

SPICY PULLED PORK WITH RED ONION CHUTNEY

Preparation time: 10 minutes, plus marinating
Cooking time: 16 hours
Serves 8

2kg (4lb 7oz) pork shoulder (off-the bone)

1 tbsp dried chilli flakes

1 tsp dried oregano

2 tbsp soft dark brown sugar, plus extra to taste

1 tsp sea salt

1 tsp chipotle chilli (smoked chilli) paste (optional)

100ml (3½fl oz) red wine vinegar

2 red onions, peeled and finely sliced

6 garlic cloves, peeled and sliced

Sea salt and freshly ground black pepper

This simple recipe tastes great!

Place the pork in a dish and rub the meat with the chilli flakes, oregano, half the sugar, salt, chilli paste (if using) and vinegar. Cover and marinate in the fridge for at least 4 hours or for up to 24 hours.

Place the remaining sugar, onions and garlic in the base of the slow cooker dish and mix well. Top with the marinated pork. Cover with the lid and cook on low for 16 hours.

Remove the pork from the slow cooker and place on a platter or board. Use 2 forks to shred the meat, discarding any large pieces of fat. Moisten the meat with the pan juices.

Season the onions in the slow cooker and add sugar to taste. Serve the pork in crusty rolls or wraps with the red onion chutney and some rocket leaves.

FAB FOR THE FREEZER
Place the shredded pork and onion chutney in separate freezerproof containers and freeze for up to three months. Defrost thoroughly before using at room temperature, or reheat gently on the hob until piping hot.

TRADITIONAL-STYLE PORK VINDALOO

Preparation time: 15 minutes
Cooking time: 8–9 hours
Serves 4

2 medium onions, peeled and finely sliced

500g (1lb 2oz) pork fillet, whole

250ml (9fl oz) hot vegetable stock

FOR THE SPICE PASTE:

½–1 tsp dried chilli flakes, to taste

1 tsp cumin seeds

½ tsp black peppercorns

½ tsp cardamom seeds, about 15 pods

½ tsp ground cinnamon

½ tsp whole black mustard seeds

½ tsp fenugreek seeds

½ tbsp ground coriander

½ tsp turmeric

200ml (7fl oz) port

½ tsp sea salt

2 tsp dark brown muscovado sugar

2 garlic cloves, peeled and crushed

2.5cm (1in) cube fresh root ginger, peeled and finely diced

You'll be pleased you made your own, but if you really don't have time to make the spice paste, use 3–4 tablespoons of ready-made vindaloo paste, available from most supermarkets.

To make the spice paste, grind the chilli flakes, cumin seeds, peppercorns, cardamom seeds, cinnamon, black mustard seeds, fenugreek seeds, coriander and turmeric in a food processor or in a mortar with a pestle until a fine powder forms.

Transfer the ground spices to a small bowl and add the port, salt, sugar, garlic and ginger. Mix well and set aside.

Arrange the onions in a single layer in the slow cooker dish. Place the pork on top and pour over the spice mix and stock.

Cover with the lid and cook on low for 8–9 hours or until the pork is tender. Remove the pork from the slow cooker dish with tongs and place on a board or plate. Using two forks, shred the meat into large pieces. Return the pork to the slow cooker dish and mix well to coat in the sauce. Serve with freshly cooked basmati rice and a cucumber and mint raita.

LAMB TAGINE WITH FRUIT AND HONEY

This easy lamb tagine is packed with the authentic flavours of Morocco, but uses simple everyday ingredients.

Place the meat and onion in the slow cooker dish together with the spices and mix well to coat, then pour over the water. Cover with the lid and cook on low for 6–8 hours or until the meat is wonderfully tender.

Increase the heat to high. Scatter over the prunes and apricots and fold in carefully to avoid breaking up the meat. Cover again and cook for a further 30–60 minutes or until the fruit is very soft. Season to taste with the honey and salt and pepper. Serve with couscous.

I ALSO LIKE...
to cook a whole lamb leg, shoulder or shanks with the same spice rub, adjusting the cooking times accordingly.

Preparation time: 10 minutes
Cooking time: 6½–9 hours
Serves 6

1.2kg (2lb 12oz) lamb, either neck, shoulder, leg or a mixture, cut into 3–4cm (1¼–1½in) chunks

1 onion, peeled and cut into 3–4cm (1¼–1½in) chunks

½ tsp ground ginger

A large pinch of saffron strands

1 tsp ground coriander

½ tsp ground cinnamon

1¼ tsp crushed dried chilli

100ml (3½fl oz) water

100g (3½oz) ready-to-eat dried prunes

100g (3½oz) ready-to-eat dried apricots

1–2 tsp runny honey (or try orange blossom honey), or to taste

Sea salt and freshly ground black pepper

ROGAN JOSH LAMB SHANKS IN DARK ALMOND SAUCE

Preparation time: 15 minutes
Cooking time: 10¼ hours
Serves 4

4 lamb shanks

4 tbsp vegetable oil

10 whole cloves

1 whole dried chilli

10 black peppercorns

10 whole cardamom pods

1 tbsp ground cumin

1 tbsp ground coriander

1 tbsp desiccated coconut

4 tbsp ground almonds

2 garlic cloves, peeled and crushed

1 tsp ground ginger

½ tsp turmeric

½ tsp sea salt

About 100ml (3½fl oz) cold water

1 x 400g (14oz) tin chopped tomatoes

If you like a mellow, medium-spiced curry then this is the one for you!

Rinse the lamb shanks under cold running water and pat dry with kitchen paper. Warm three-quarters of the vegetable oil in a large frying pan over a medium heat. When hot, add the cloves, chilli, peppercorns and cardamom pods and cook for about 30 seconds or until they become dark and fragrant. Remove with a slotted spoon and set aside.

Return the pan to the heat, add the lamb and cook for 5–10 minutes or until browned all over. Remove the meat from the pan with tongs and place in the slow cooker dish.

Return the pan to the heat again and reduce the temperature to medium. Add the cumin, coriander, coconut, almonds and garlic, mix well and cook until the mixture turns a dark gold colour. Remove from the heat and add the ginger, turmeric and salt.

Spoon the mixture into a food processor together with the reserved whole spices and the water and blitz until a smooth paste forms. Add to the slow cooker dish together with the tomatoes and stir well to coat the lamb in the sauce. Cover with the lid and cook on low for 10 hours.

Remove the dish from the base and place on a heatproof surface. Skim off any excess fat with a spoon. Place the shanks on warm serving dishes with plenty of sauce spooned over the top and serve with freshly cooked rice.

JAMAICAN LAMB CURRY

Preparation time: 20 minutes
Cooking time: 6¼ –8¼ Hours
Serves 6

2 tbsp vegetable oil

800g (1lb 12oz) lamb shoulder, cut into 4cm (1½in) chunks

1 large onion, peeled and cut into chunks

2 sweet potatoes, peeled and cut into chunks

1 red pepper, deseeded and cut into chunks

2 green chillies, roughly chopped (deseeded if you prefer a milder curry)

5cm (2in) piece fresh root ginger, peeled and grated

¼ tsp ground nutmeg

1 tsp ground allspice

Juice of 2 limes

2–3 tbsp dark brown muscovado sugar, or to taste

15g (½oz) fresh flat-leaf parsley, finely chopped

I love the warming combinations of spices in Caribbean cooking. I have used lamb in this fragrant recipe, but goat would be even more authentic if you can get it.

Warm the vegetable oil in a large frying pan over a high heat. When hot, add the lamb in 2–3 batches and cook until browned all over, spooning the cooked batches into the slow cooker dish with a slotted spoon.

Return the frying pan to the heat, add the onion and cook for 5 minutes or until starting to colour. Transfer them to the slow cooker dish, then stir in all the remaining ingredients, except the parsley. Cover with the lid and cook on low for 6–8 hours or until the meat and potatoes are tender.

Stir in the parsley and serve with freshly cooked rice or crusty bread.

I ALSO LIKE...
to make this curry with chicken pieces on the bone, cooking them for a maximum of 6 hours.

LAMB MASSAMAN CURRY

This rich, creamy curry is wonderfully aromatic and spicy. Massaman paste is available at most major supermarkets.

Pour the coconut milk into the slow cooker dish and mix in the massaman paste. Add the lamb and the vegetables and mix well.

Cover with the lid and cook on low for 8–9 hours or until the lamb is tender and the sauce has thickened slightly.

Add the fish sauce to taste, then garnish with coriander leaves and serve with lime wedges for squeezing over accompanied with freshly cooked rice or noodles.

I ALSO LIKE...
to make a vegetarian version using sweet potato or squash in place of the lamb. Check the curry paste you're using though as some brands have shrimp paste as an ingredient and are not suitable for vegetarians.

Preparation time: 10 minutes
Cooking time: 8–9 hours
Serves 4

1 x 400ml (14fl oz) tin coconut milk

5–6 tsp massaman curry paste

600g (1lb 5oz) lamb shoulder, cut into chunks

1 onion, peeled, halved and finely sliced

1 aubergine, cut into chunks

1 red pepper, deseeded and cut into chunks

250g (9oz) baby new potatoes, washed and halved

2–3 tbsp fish sauce, to taste

Fresh coriander leaves, to garnish

Lime wedges, to serve

EASY BEEF BIRYANI

I love biriyanis, and this version is seriously easy and perfect for all the family.

Warm the vegetable oil in a large frying pan over a high heat. When hot, add the meat and cook for 5–10 minutes or until well browned all over.

Place the meat in the slow cooker dish together with the rice, lentils, tomatoes and curry sauce. Half fill the jar with cold water and rinse out into the slow cooker dish. Cover with the lid and cook on low for 3–4 hours or until both the meat and rice are tender.

Stir the mango chutney gently through the mixture, trying to avoid breaking up the meat, and sprinkle coriander over the top before serving with raita and naan bread.

I ALSO LIKE...
to use 600g (1lb 5oz) beef mince instead of braising steak.

Preparation time: 10 minutes
Cooking time: 3¼–4¼ hours
Serves 4

1 tbsp vegetable oil

600g (1lb 5oz) stewing or braising steak, cut into 1–2cm (½–¾in) pieces

150g (5oz) basmati rice, rinsed and drained

150g (5oz) red lentils, rinsed and drained

2 tomatoes, chopped

1 x 425g jar good-quality balti curry sauce

4 tbsp good-quality mango chutney

A small handful of fresh coriander leaves, to serve

MOGUL LAMB WITH SAFFRON AND RAISINS

Preparation time: 15 minutes
Cooking time: 6¼–8¼ hours, plus resting
Serves 6

2 tbsp vegetable oil

1kg (2lb 4oz) lamb neck or shoulder, cut into 3–4cm (1¼–1½in) pieces

2 onions, peeled and cut into cubes

5 garlic cloves, peeled and sliced

5cm (2in) piece fresh root ginger, peeled and shredded

A large pinch of saffron strands

½ tsp chilli flakes, or to taste

1 tbsp ground coriander

2 tsp ground cumin

½ tsp ground cloves

½ tsp ground cinnamon

2 tbsp seedless raisins

Sea salt and freshly ground black pepper

2 tbsp finely chopped fresh flat-leaf parsley

I love this fragrant Middle Eastern-inspired dish. It's amazing with lamb, but also works with chicken if you'd rather – cook the chicken on the bone, though, to stop it from drying out.

Warm the vegetable oil in a large frying pan over a high heat. When hot, add the meat, in batches if necessary, and cook for about 5–10 minutes or until well browned. Transfer the meat to the slow cooker dish with a slotted spoon.

Add all the remaining ingredients except the raisins, seasoning and parsley to the slow cooker dish and mix to combine. Cover with the lid and cook on low for 6–8 hours or until the meat is wonderfully tender.

Remove the slow cooker dish from the base and place on a heatproof surface. Scatter the raisins over the lamb and cover again with the lid. Leave to rest for 10 minutes.

Season with salt and pepper and add the parsley, then mix very gently, being careful not to break up the meat. Serve with couscous or rice.

I ALSO LIKE...
making this recipe with a whole bone-in shoulder of lamb. Cook for at least 8 hours or for up to 12 hours until the meat is falling off the bone.

BEEF WITH WHOLE SPICES

Don't be put off by the long list of ingredients; this is the easiest dish to make, and tastes SO good.

Rinse the meat under cold running water and pat dry with kitchen paper. Arrange the onion in a single layer over the base of the slow cooker dish.

Warm the vegetable oil in a large, deep, heavy-based frying pan over a medium heat. When very hot, add the whole spices and cook for about 1 minute or until just coloured and fragrant. Add the beef, in batches if necessary, and cook for about 5 minutes or until browned all over. Add the ginger and salt and mix well, then spoon the contents of the pan, including the oil, into the slow cooker dish. Pour over the stock. Cover with the lid and cook on low for 4-6 hours or until tender.

Remove the beef and spices with a slotted spoon and place in a serving dish. Sprinkle the garam masala and chilli slices over the top. Serve with rice, thick natural yoghurt and naan bread.

COOKING CONVENTIONALLY?
Cook in an ovenproof casserole dish with a tight-fitting lid in an oven preheated to 150°C (300°F), Gas mark 2, for 2-3 hours or until tender.

Preparation time: 15 minutes
Cooking time: 4¼-6¼ hours
Serves 4-6

1kg (2lb 4oz) thick-cut feather steak slices or braising steak slices

1 large onion, peeled and finely sliced

6 tbsp vegetable oil

1 cinnamon stick

10 whole black peppercorns

15 whole cloves

15 whole cardamom pods

2 star anise

2 bay leaves

1 whole dried chilli

2cm (¾in) piece fresh root ginger, peeled and shredded

½ tsp sea salt

250ml (9fl oz) hot beef stock

2 tsp garam masala

Sliced green chilli, for sprinkling

CHOCOLATE CHILLI CON CARNE

Preparation time: 15 minutes
Cooking time: 6¾ hours
Serves 4

500g (1lb 2oz) lean beef mince

1 tbsp olive oil

1 large red onion, peeled and diced

1 red pepper, deseeded and diced

2 garlic cloves, peeled and crushed

1 heaped tsp hot chilli powder (or less for a milder chilli)

1 tsp paprika

1 tsp ground cumin

1 beef stock cube

1 x 400g (14oz) tin chopped tomatoes

2 tbsp tomato purée

A pinch of dried thyme

1 x 410g (14oz) tin red kidney beans, drained and rinsed

1 square of good-quality plain dark chocolate (at least 70% cocoa solids)

Sea salt and freshly ground black pepper

I love this recipe! The chocolate adds a richness and roundness of flavour to the finished dish.

Pat the mince dry with kitchen paper. Warm the olive oil in a large frying pan over a high heat. When hot, add the onion and pepper and cook for 5 minutes or until softened and golden. Add the garlic, chilli, paprika and cumin, stir well and cook, stirring occasionally, for a further 5 minutes. Reduce the heat if anything threatens to burn.

Spoon the vegetables into the slow cooker dish. Return the frying pan to the high heat and, when very hot, add the mince and cook for about 5–10 minutes, stirring well until the mince has broken up and has browned. Spoon the mince into the slow cooker dish.

Crumble the stock cube over the mince and vegetables and mix together with the tomatoes, tomato purée and thyme. Cover with the lid and cook on low for 6 hours or until tender.

Stir in the beans, cover again and cook for a further 30 minutes or until piping hot.

Add the chocolate and season to taste with salt and pepper. Serve with soured cream and plenty of freshly cooked rice.

BRAISES, STEWS
+
OTHER COMFORT
FOOD

VEGETARIAN SHEPHERD'S PIE WITH CELERIAC AND CHEDDAR TOPPING

Preparation time: 20 minutes
Cooking time: 6¼–8¼ hours
Serves 6
Vegetarian

1 large red onion, peeled and chopped

2 carrots, peeled and diced

500g (1lb 2oz) parsnips, peeled and diced

200ml (7fl oz) red wine (preferably vegetarian)

1 tbsp chopped fresh rosemary leaves

1 x 400g (14oz) tin chopped tomatoes

200g (7oz) Puy or green lentils, rinsed and drained

250ml (9fl oz) vegetable stock

Sea salt and freshly ground white pepper

FOR THE TOPPING:

850g (1lb 14oz) celeriac, peeled and roughly chopped

350g (12oz) potatoes, peeled and roughly chopped

75g (3oz) grated mature Cheddar cheese

There is no reason why a meat eater should feel hard done by when eating this shepherd's pie – it just happens to be vegetarian!

Place all of the ingredients except for the seasoning and the topping in the slow cooker dish. Mix well but do not season at this stage, as salt will toughen the lentils. Cover with the lid and cook on low for 6–8 hours or until thickened.

When you get home from work or 30 minutes before you are ready to eat, cook the celeriac and potato pieces in a large saucepan of boiling water for 10–15 minutes or until tender. Drain thoroughly and return to the pan. Add two-thirds of the cheese and mash well until completely smooth. Season to taste with salt and pepper.

If your slow cooker dish is flameproof (see manufacturer's instructions), preheat the grill to its highest setting. Season the lentil mixture in the slow cooker to taste and spoon the mashed celeriac mixture evenly over the top to cover the lentils completely.

Sprinkle the remaining cheese over the top of the mash and cook under the grill for 5–10 minutes or until golden brown. Allow to cool for about 5 minutes before serving with seasonal green vegetables or salad.

FAB FOR THE FREEZER
Spoon the cooked lentil mixture into individual portion freezerproof containers, allowing to cool, then top with the mash and freeze for those days when cooking is not an option. Reheat from frozen in an oven preheated to 180°C (350°F), Gas mark 4 for 30–40 minutes or until hot.

BLACK BEAN GUMBO

This gumbo is spicy in a warming and soothing way, but is definitely hot, so if you like something a little bit milder just add less white pepper.

Soak the beans in a bowl of cold water overnight. The next day, drain and place in the slow cooker dish.

Add the onion and celery to the dish together with the garlic and chillies, then add the remaining ingredients except the salt and spinach and mix well.

Cover with the lid and cook on low for 8 hours. Season to taste with the reserved salt and stir in the spinach just before serving with tortillas or freshly cooked long-grain rice.

I ALSO LIKE...
using other dried beans; but if you use red kidney beans you must soak them overnight and boil according to the packet instructions before use.

Preparation time: 5 minutes, plus soaking

Cooking time: 8 hours

Serves 4

Vegetarian

200g (7oz) dried black beans or black-eyed beans

1 red onion, peeled and finely chopped

2 celery sticks, trimmed and finely chopped

2 garlic cloves, peeled and crushed

2 red chillies, deseeded and finely chopped

150ml (5fl oz) vegetable stock

2 x 400g (14oz) tins chopped tomatoes

1 tsp dried thyme

1 tsp cayenne pepper

1 tsp dried oregano

¼–½ tsp white pepper

½ tsp sea salt

200g (7oz) baby spinach leaves, washed

WINTER VEGETABLE STEW WITH THYME DUMPLINGS

Preparation time: 10 minutes
Cooking time: 4½–6½ hours
Serves 4
Vegetarian

2 large waxy potatoes, peeled and cut into chunks

2 tbsp plain flour

1 onion, peeled and cut into chunks

1 leek, trimmed and cut into chunks

3 carrots, peeled and cut into chunks

2 celery sticks, trimmed and cut into chunks

75g (3oz) pearl barley

2 fresh thyme sprigs

250ml (9fl oz) dry cider or apple juice

250ml (9fl oz) hot vegetable stock or water

Sea salt and freshly ground black pepper

FOR THE THYME DUMPLINGS:

150g (5oz) self-raising flour

75g (3oz) vegetable suet

1 tbsp fresh thyme leaves

About 100ml (4fl oz) cold water

Vegetarians seem to miss out on hearty stew-like fare, which is often monopolised by gutsy meat dishes. This recipe ticks all the hearty, warming, comfort food boxes that you'd expect from the best of winter stews. Make sure your slow cooker dish can be used in the oven before making this recipe.

Place the potatoes in the slow cooker dish and mix with the flour. Scatter the vegetables and pearl barley into the slow cooker so that they completely cover the potato (if the potato is in contact with the air it will turn brown). Add the thyme and pour over the cider or apple juice and stock (it should just cover the vegetables). Cover with the lid and cook on low for 4–6 hours or until the vegetables are tender and the sauce is thickened.

Mix the stew and season to taste with salt and pepper. At this point, make the dumplings (check that your slow cooker dish can be used in the oven first).

Preheat the oven to 200°C (400°F), Gas mark 6. Mix the flour, suet and thyme together in a large bowl and season to taste. Add enough water to form a firm dough. Drop 8 large spoonfuls of the dough into the hot stew, pushing them in so they are only just poking out.

Place the slow cooker dish in the oven and cook, uncovered, for 20 minutes or until the dumplings are golden and cooked through. Serve with seasonal greens and mash.

I ALSO LIKE...

to make a meaty chicken version of this stew. Brown some chicken pieces in a hot frying pan with a little olive or vegetable oil until just golden, then add them to the slow cooker with the vegetables and barley at the beginning.

ROSTI-TOPPED FISH PIE

Fish is usually best cooked very quickly to retain its moist texture. In this instance, cooking the fish in a tasty tomato sauce retains its succulence while allowing its flavours to develop and combine with the sauce to make a fantastic pie.

Place the fish in the slow cooker dish with the seafood.

Add the tomatoes, tomato purée, vermouth (if using), dill and garlic. Season generously with salt and pepper and mix gently to combine.

Peel and coarsely grate the potatoes into a large bowl. Drizzle the lemon juice over and mix well. Pour the melted butter over the top and mix again. Season well and spoon the topping evenly over the tomato mixture until completely covered.

Cover with the lid and cook on low for 3 hours or until the potato is tender.

If your slow cooker dish is flameproof (see manufacturer's instructions), preheat the grill to its highest setting and place the dish under the grill for 5–10 minutes or until golden brown. Serve immediately with peas.

I ALSO LIKE...
using other firm-fleshed fish, such as smoked haddock.

Preparation time: 10 minutes
Cooking time: 3¼ hours
Serves 4

500g (1lb 2oz) firm white fish fillets, such as cod, haddock or pollack, cut into 4cm (1½in) pieces

200g (7oz) mixed ready-to-eat, cooked seafood, such as prawns, calamari or mussels

1 x 400g (14oz) tin chopped tomatoes

1 tbsp tomato purée

50ml (1¾fl oz) vermouth (optional)

2 tbsp finely chopped fresh dill

1 garlic clove, peeled and crushed

Sea salt and freshly ground black pepper

3–4 large potatoes, about 850g (1lb 14oz) in total

Juice of ½ lemon

50g (2oz) butter, melted and cooled slightly

HOT-SMOKED SALMON AND POTATO BAKE

Preparation time: 10 minutes
Cooking time: 2 hours
Serves 4 as a light main course

500g (1lb 2oz) waxy potatoes, unpeeled and thinly sliced into 5mm (¼in) discs

200g (7oz) hot-smoked salmon fillets, skin removed

3 fresh tarragon sprigs

Finely grated zest of ½ lemon (preferably unwaxed)

Sea salt and freshly ground black pepper

300ml (10fl oz) double cream

200ml (7fl oz) semi-skimmed milk

This gloriously rich and fragrant dish is utterly wonderful. Serve warm as opposed to hot or cold to allow the flavours to be at their best.

Arrange one-third of the potatoes in a single layer in the base of a shallow baking dish that is just smaller than your slow cooker dish (this recipe will fit a 1.5 litre/2½ pint oval baking dish).

Flake half of the salmon over the potatoes followed by half of both the tarragon and lemon zest. Season generously with pepper.

Repeat this process once again finishing with a final layer of overlapping potato slices – this is the only layer that will be seen, so it is worth taking a little trouble over it to make it look pretty.

Mix the cream and milk together in a jug, then pour gently and gradually over the potatoes, allowing it to seep down into the depths of the dish between each addition. Ensure that the potato is completely covered in cream, then season the top with a little salt and more pepper. Place the baking dish in the slow cooker dish and carefully pour cold water around the outside to come about halfway up the sides of the baking dish. Cover with the lid and cook on high for 2 hours or until the potatoes are tender.

Preheat the grill to its highest setting. Remove the baking dish from the slow cooker and place it under the grill for 2–3 minutes until the top is golden. Serve immediately with a green salad or some seasonal green vegetables.

SWEET AND SOY GINGER CHICKEN

Everyone seems to love this chicken dish – and as a bonus it's really easy and cheap to make too!

Mix the soy sauce, sugar, garlic, chopped coriander, ginger, cornflour, half of the spring onions, the vinegar and ground coriander together in the slow cooker dish.

Add the chicken and mix well to coat in the soy mixture. Cover with the lid and cook on low for about 6 hours or until the chicken is tender and there is no pink meat.

Skim off and discard any fat from the surface of the cooking liquid. Scatter the remaining spring onions and some coriander leaves over the chicken before serving with freshly cooked rice.

I ALSO LIKE...
making this recipe with pork spareribs.

Preparation time: 10 minutes
Cooking time: 6 hours
Serves 4

75ml (2½fl oz) light soy sauce

2 tbsp dark brown muscovado sugar

4 garlic cloves, peeled and thinly sliced

A large handful of fresh coriander, finely chopped, plus extra leaves to serve

5cm (2in) piece fresh root ginger, peeled and cut into thin strips

1 tbsp cornflour

4 spring onions, trimmed and finely sliced on the diagonal

1 tbsp sherry vinegar, rice wine or white wine vinegar

1 tsp ground coriander

8 chicken drumsticks

PAPRIKA CHICKEN WITH CHORIZO

Preparation time: 15 minutes
Cooking time: 4½–6½ hours
Serves 4

1 medium chicken, cut into 8 pieces on the bone

1–2 tsp smoked paprika

Sea salt and freshly ground black pepper

1 tbsp olive oil

100g (3½oz) chorizo, cut into chunks

1 onion, peeled and cut into chunks

1 red pepper, deseeded and cut into chunks

1 green pepper, deseeded and cut into chunks

4 garlic cloves, peeled and finely sliced

200ml (7fl oz) chicken stock

1 x 400g (14oz) tin chopped tomatoes

2 tbsp concentrated tomato purée

2 tbsp soured cream

This is one of my favourite recipes in this book – it's so easy to make and packed with flavour.

Wash the chicken pieces under cold running water and pat dry with kitchen paper. Place the paprika and some salt and pepper in a large freezer bag. Add the chicken, seal the top and shake to coat the chicken in the powder.

Warm the olive oil in a large frying pan over a high heat. When hot, add the chorizo and cook for about a minute or until the orangey oil is released. Remove with a slotted spoon and place in the slow cooker dish. Return the pan to the heat, add the chicken together with any remaining paprika and cook for 5–10 minutes or until golden all over. Remove with a slotted spoon and transfer to the slow cooker.

Return the pan to the heat once again and add the onion, peppers and garlic. Stir-fry for about 5 minutes or until softened. Tip into the slow cooker together with any oil in the pan and mix well.

Pour over the stock, tomatoes and tomato purée. Cover with the lid and cook on low for 4–6 hours or until the chicken is tender and there is no pink meat.

Remove the slow cooker dish from the heat and add the soured cream. Leave it to melt into the sauce before serving. Great with chunky bread and a dressed green salad.

AROMATIC CHICKEN WITH LEMON

Preparation time: 20 minutes
Cooking time: 6¼–8¼ hours
Serves 4

8 mixed chicken pieces on the bone,
such as legs, thighs and drumsticks,
or joint a whole chicken

Sea salt and freshly ground black
pepper

1 tbsp olive oil

25g (1oz) butter

2 large onions, peeled and finely
sliced

2 garlic cloves, peeled and crushed

1 tsp ground cinnamon

1 tsp ground ginger

2 lemons (preferably unwaxed)

About 150ml (5fl oz) cold water

2 tbsp roughly chopped fresh
flat-leaf parsley

**This simple dish is wonderfully tasty, and equally at home for
the family during the week or for guests when entertaining.**

Season the chicken pieces with salt and pepper. Warm the olive
oil and butter in a large frying pan over a high heat. When hot,
add the chicken and cook for about 5 minutes or until golden
on both sides.

Place the onions in the slow cooker dish together with the garlic
and spices. Arrange the chicken in a single layer over the top and
pour over any cooking juices. Finely grate the lemon zest over
the chicken and squeeze over the juice, then pour in enough of
the water to come halfway up the sides of the chicken. Cover
with the lid and cook on low for 6–8 hours or until the chicken
is tender and the sauce has thickened.

Sprinkle over the parsley and serve with couscous, rice or mash.

FAB FOR THE FREEZER
Leave the chicken to cool completely before spooning into
airtight containers and freezing for up to three months. Defrost
thoroughly before reheating gently on the hob (never in the slow
cooker).

SPRING CHICKEN AND VEGETABLE CASSEROLE

Your slow cooker needn't be put away as soon as winter ends. This yummy spring casserole is enough encouragement to keep it cooking throughout the year.

Warm the olive oil in a large frying pan over a high heat. Season the chicken legs with salt and pepper, then cook skin side down until golden. Transfer the chicken to the slow cooker dish with a slotted spoon.

Return the frying pan to the heat. Add the shallots and fry for 3–5 minutes or until golden. Add to the slow cooker together with the fennel, potatoes, carrots, bay leaves, thyme and tomato purée and mix well.

Pour over the cider or apple juice. Cover with the lid and cook on low for 4–6 hours or until the chicken is tender and there is no pink meat.

Just before serving stir in the spinach and some extra seasoning to taste. Spoon into deep plates or bowls and serve with mash or crusty bread.

Preparation time: **15 minutes**
Cooking time: **4¼–6¼ hours**
Serves **4**

2 tbsp olive oil

4 chicken legs

Sea salt and freshly ground black pepper

12–16 shallots, halved and peeled

2 small fennel bulbs, trimmed and cut into wedges

150g (5oz) baby new potatoes, washed

200g (7oz) baby carrots, washed and halved lengthways

2 bay leaves

4 fresh thyme sprigs

1 tbsp concentrated tomato purée

500ml (18fl oz) dry cider or apple juice

150–200g (5–7oz) baby spinach leaves

COUNTRY CHICKEN WITH LEEKS, CREAM AND BACON

Preparation time: 15–20 minutes
Cooking time: 6½ hours
Serves 4–6

1 whole medium chicken, cut into 8 pieces, such as drumsticks, thighs and each breast cut in half on the bone

Sea salt and freshly ground black pepper

25g (1oz) butter

1 tbsp olive oil

50g (2oz) plain flour

25g (1oz) smoked streaky bacon, diced

1 tbsp fresh tarragon leaves

450g (1lb) thin leeks, trimmed and cut into 3cm (1¼in) lengths

200ml (7fl oz) dry cider or apple juice

150ml (5fl oz) crème fraîche

The combination of chicken with cream, bacon, tarragon and leeks is just about perfect, and this recipe is no exception.

Rinse the chicken under cold running water and pat dry with kitchen paper. Season the chicken with salt and pepper.

Warm the butter and olive oil in a large frying pan over a high heat. When hot, add half the chicken pieces, skin side down, and cook for 5–10 minutes, until golden. Transfer the chicken pieces to the slow cooker dish. Repeat this process with the remaining chicken. When all the chicken is browned, and in the slow cooker dish, sprinkle over the flour and mix well until all the pieces are evenly coated.

Return the pan to the heat and add the bacon. Cook for 5 minutes or until just golden. Scatter the bacon and any cooking juices over the chicken together with the tarragon.

Rinse the leeks under cold running water. Drain well and arrange them in a layer over the chicken. Pour over the cider or apple juice. Cover with the lid and cook on low for 6 hours or until the chicken is tender and there is no pink meat.

Add the crème fraîche and gently stir into the sauce, being careful not to break up the chicken pieces. Serve with rice or mash and plenty of seasonal green vegetables.

SUMMER SAUSAGE BRAISE

Preparation time: 15 minutes

Cooking time: 6¼ hours

Serves 6

1 tbsp olive oil

12 good-quality pork and herb sausages

12 baby shallots, peeled

200g (7oz) smoked streaky bacon, diced

2 celery sticks, trimmed and chopped

2 garlic cloves, peeled and crushed

500g (1lb 2oz) cherry tomatoes

100ml (3½fl oz) dry white wine

100ml (3½fl oz) vegetable stock

Sea salt and freshly ground black pepper

25g (1oz) fresh basil

This braise is great family food and ideal for an easy, economical mid-week supper.

Warm the olive oil in a large frying pan over a medium heat. When hot, add the sausages and cook for 5–10 minutes or until browned. Spoon them into the slow cooker dish.

Return the pan to the heat and add the shallots and bacon and cook for 5 minutes or until golden. Add them to the sausages in the slow cooker.

Mix in the celery, garlic, tomatoes, wine and stock. Cover with the lid and cook on low for 6 hours or until the sauce is thick.

Season to taste with salt and pepper. Rip the basil and scatter it over the sausages. Serve with crusty bread and salad.

FAB FOR THE FREEZER

Leave to cool thoroughly, then place in an airtight plastic container and keep in the freezer for up to three months. Defrost fully before reheating gently on the hob (never in the slow cooker)

EASY PORK CASSOULET

Preparation time: 5 minutes

Cooking time: 6–8 hours

Serves 4

500g (1lb 2oz) diced pork shoulder

1 onion, peeled and diced

2 rashers streaky bacon, diced

2 tbsp tomato purée

2 garlic cloves, peeled and finely sliced

1 x 400g (14oz) tin chopped tomatoes

1 x 410g (14oz) tin cannellini beans, drained and rinsed

1 tbsp caster sugar, to taste

Sea salt and freshly ground black pepper

1 tbsp chopped fresh flat-leaf parsley

Cassoulet is such a rich and rewarding dish and it really benefits from slow cooking. This easy version does cut some corners but still produces a fantastic result for those with less time for preparation – it's also really economical to make.

Throw everything other than the parsley into the slow cooker dish and mix well.

Cover with the lid and cook on low for 6 hours or for up to 8 hours.

Season to taste with salt and pepper. Spoon into shallow bowls and sprinkle with the chopped parsley. Serve with plenty of crusty bread and a green salad.

FAB FOR THE FREEZER

Make a double batch and freeze in portions – perfect ready meals for those days when you don't feel like cooking.

24-HOUR HUNGARIAN PORK

Try this wonderfully tasty and moist pork dish – perfect for a main course, or also great hot or cold in sandwiches.

Rinse the pork under cold running water and pat dry with kitchen paper. Place in the slow cooker dish.

Place the garlic, paprika, chilli flakes, caraway seeds, sugar, salt, tomato purée and water into a food processor and blitz to make a thick paste. Alternatively, use a pestle and mortar. Rub the paste all over the pork. Cover with the lid and cook on low for 24 hours or until gloriously tender.

Remove the pork from the slow cooker and place on a plate or board. Use 2 forks to remove any large pieces of fat and discard. Use the forks to divide the meat into large pieces.

Skim off any excess fat from the surface of the cooking liquid. Stir in the soured cream and season to taste with salt and pepper. Drizzle the cooking juices over the meat before serving with new potatoes and salad.

FAB FOR THE FREEZER
Leave the meat to cool in the sauce without adding the soured cream. The fat will harden, making it easier to remove. Freeze the meat for up to three months. Defrost thoroughly, before reheating in the sauce gently on the hob until piping hot. Add the soured cream and stir through.

Preparation time: 10 minutes
Cooking time: 24 hours
Serves 8

3 kg (6lb 8oz) bone-in shoulder of pork (or a size to fit in your slow cooker dish)

5 garlic cloves, peeled

2 tsp smoked paprika

A large pinch of dried chilli flakes, or to taste

1 tsp caraway seeds

1 tbsp dark brown muscovado sugar

½ tsp sea salt

2 tbsp concentrated tomato purée

4 tbsp cold water

5 tbsp soured cream

Sea salt and freshly ground black pepper

LEMON AND HONEY PORK CHOPS

Preparation time: 10 minutes
Cooking time: 4¼–6¼ hours
Serves 6

1 tbsp olive oil

6 thick-cut, bone-in pork chops (with fat)

2 red onions, peeled and finely sliced

12 garlic cloves, peeled

2 fresh thyme sprigs, leaves only

1 lemon, cut into chunks

Sea salt and freshly ground black pepper

150ml (5fl oz) pork, vegetable or chicken stock

125g (4½oz) clear honey

A small handful of fresh oregano leaves

You might think that the lemon chunks would be overpowering in this recipe, but instead they become caramelised and really make this dish.

Warm the olive oil in a large frying pan over a high heat. When hot, add the chops and cook briefly until browned on each side.

Place the onions in the slow cooker dish and scatter over the garlic and thyme. Top with the chops. Tuck the lemon chunks in between the meat and season with salt and pepper, before drizzling over the stock and the honey. Cover with the lid and cook on low for 4–6 hours or until the pork is tender and the onions are soft.

Season to taste and mix everything together. Scatter the oregano leaves over the top before serving with mash or new potatoes.

I ALSO LIKE...
to cook a pork shoulder roast in the same way, adjusting the cooking time accordingly to about 8 hours on low (depending on weight).

PORK WITH BRAISED RED CABBAGE AND APPLE

Preparation time: 10 minutes
Cooking time: 6¼–8¼ hours
Serves 6

25g (1oz) butter

1 large onion, peeled and finely sliced

½ tsp ground allspice

¼ tsp freshly grated nutmeg

1 small red cabbage, cored and finely sliced

1 Bramley apple, peeled, cored and diced

4 tbsp red wine vinegar

2 tbsp light muscovado sugar

100ml (3½fl oz) cold water

Sea salt and freshly ground black pepper

1–1.5kg (2lb 4oz–3lb 5oz) pork shoulder

2 tbsp redcurrant jelly

This warming winter dish is actually really good in the summer months too and is great served with steamed green beans or broccoli.

Melt the butter in a pan over a medium heat, add the onion and cook for 5 minutes or until softened but not browned. Spoon into the slow cooker dish.

Stir the spices into the slow cooker dish, then add the cabbage, apple, red wine vinegar, sugar and cold water. Stir until thoroughly mixed and the sugar has dissolved. Season generously with salt and pepper. Top with the pork and push down – the cooker will be really full at this point and may need some coaxing to get the lid on! Cover with the lid and cook on low for 6–8 hours.

Remove the meat and leave it to rest. Alternatively, if you like crackling, preheat the grill to its highest setting and cook skin side up for about 3 minutes or until crisp and puffed-up. Stir the redcurrant jelly into the cabbage and season to taste.

Carve the meat into thick slices and serve on a bed of cabbage with any cooking juices drizzled over.

ORANGE BRAISED LAMB

The rounded citrus flavour of the orange works really well to cut through the richness of the lamb in this dish.

Wash the lamb under cold running water and pat dry on kitchen paper. Warm half of the olive oil in a large frying pan over a high heat. When hot, add the carrot and celery and cook for 5 minutes or until softened but not coloured. Using a slotted spoon transfer to the slow cooker dish. Return the pan to the heat and add the remaining oil. When hot, add the lamb and cook for 5–10 minutes or until browned all over (do this in batches). Transfer the meat to the slow cooker with a slotted spoon.

Return the pan to the heat again and add the wine. Stir vigorously to scrape up any bits from the bottom of the pan, then add to the meat together with the bay leaves, rosemary and garlic.

Finely grate the zest of the oranges and place all but about 2 teaspoons of the zest in the slow cooker. Add the juice of 1½ oranges and reserve the extra zest and juice from the remaining orange half. Add the tomato purée and stock to the slow cooker and stir together well. Cover with the lid and cook on low for 6–8 hours or until the meat is tender.

Skim off any fat from the surface of the liquid. Remove the meat with a slotted spoon and keep warm. Strain the sauce through a sieve into a clean saucepan. Bring to the boil and bubble for 5–10 minutes or until reduced by half. Remove from the heat, add the reserved zest and juice and season to taste. Serve the meat with the sauce spooned over.

Preparation time: 10 minutes
Cooking time: 6½–8½ hours
Serves 4

600g (1lb 5oz) lamb neck fillet

2 tbsp olive oil

1 carrot, peeled and finely diced

2 celery sticks, trimmed and finely diced

100ml (3½fl oz) white wine

2 bay leaves, broken

2 fresh rosemary sprigs

2 garlic cloves, peeled and finely chopped

2 oranges

1 tbsp concentrated tomato purée

200ml (7fl oz) lamb or vegetable stock

Sea salt and freshly ground black pepper

FRUITY MOROCCAN LAMB SHANKS

Preparation time: **10 minutes**
Cooking time: **8 hours**
Serves **4**

4 lamb shanks

1 x 400g (14oz) tin chopped tomatoes

2 tbsp concentrated tomato purée

2 tbsp chunky apricot jam

4 garlic cloves, peeled and roughly chopped

Finely grated zest and juice of 1 orange

½ tsp ground ginger

½ tsp ground cinnamon

1 fresh rosemary sprig

600g (1lb 5oz) baby new potatoes, washed

Sea salt and freshly ground black pepper

Lamb shanks are perfect for slow cooking. Their central bone keeps the meat tender and moist and the long slow cooking helps to break down the fat and the muscle, leaving the meat meltingly tender. They go wonderfully with fruity sauces, and this one is no exception.

Rinse the lamb shanks under cold running water and pat dry with kitchen paper. Mix the tomatoes, tomato purée, jam, garlic, orange zest and juice, ginger, cinnamon and rosemary together in the slow cooker dish. Add the potatoes and lamb and mix well to coat. Pull the lamb to the surface, allowing the potatoes to fall beneath, and season the lamb well with salt and pepper. Cover with the lid and cook on low for 8 hours or until the meat and potatoes are tender.

Season again to taste before serving with seasonal greens.

I ALSO LIKE...

to use a handful of dried apricots, or when in season fresh stoned apricots if I have them. They will make the sauce thicker, though, so add a little water if you prefer.

IRISH STEW

Preparation time: 10 minutes
Cooking time: 9 hours
Serves 6–8

---

1 large onion, peeled and finely sliced

---

2 large carrots, peeled and roughly chopped

---

3 celery sticks, trimmed and roughly chopped

850g (1lb 14oz) lamb neck fillet, cut into 3cm (1¼in) chunks

---

6 tbsp pearl barley

450g (1lb) potatoes, such as Maris Piper, peeled and diced into 3cm (1¼in) chunks

---

2 x 400g (14oz) tins chopped tomatoes

Sea salt and freshly ground black pepper

Roughly chopped fresh mint and flat-leaf parsley, to serve

Far from the greasy, fatty Irish stew of school dinners of old, this fresh-tasting version is fantastic, and as good in the summer as it is in the depths of winter.

Mix the onion, carrots and celery together in a bowl. Using about a third of the vegetables, make a layer over the base of the slow cooker dish. Top with about a third of the lamb, then one-third of pearl barley and potatoes, and finally a layer of tomatoes. Season generously with salt and pepper and repeat again, twice, to make three layers, finishing with tomatoes.

Cover with the lid and cook on low for 9 hours or until the sauce has thickened and the lamb and potatoes are wonderfully tender. Sprinkle with the chopped mint and parsley before serving.

COOKING CONVENTIONALLY?
Place in a casserole dish with a tight-fitting lid in an oven preheated to 180°C (350°F), Gas mark 4 for 2–3 hours or until the lamb is tender.

EASY BEEF STEW

This comforting stew is, as the title suggests, really easy and quick to make. It doesn't require any browning or complicated preparation – you just throw it all in! It is perfect for an after-work supper or for entertaining when preparation time is limited.

Place the beef in the slow cooker dish together with the tomato purée, vinegar and flour and mix until the beef is well coated.

Add the vegetables, garlic and bay leaves to the slow cooker and mix well. Season with salt and pepper. Cover with the lid and cook on low for 8 hours or until the meat is meltingly tender.

Serve with salad or seasonal vegetables.

FAB FOR THE FREEZER
Make a double batch and freeze in portions for a day when you don't have time to cook. Defrost thoroughly before reheating gently on the hob (never in a slow cooker).

Preparation time: 15 minutes
Cooking time: 8 hours
Serves 6

1.5kg (3lb 5oz) stewing or braising steak, cut into 3–4cm (1¼ –1½in) chunks

3 tbsp concentrated tomato purée

3 tbsp balsamic vinegar

2 tbsp plain flour

2 onions, peeled and cut into 2–3cm (¾–1¼ in) chunks

2 large carrots, peeled and cut into 2–3cm (¾–1¼ in) chunks

450g (1lb) baby new potatoes, washed

3 garlic cloves, peeled and crushed

2 bay leaves, broken

Sea salt and freshly ground black pepper

ITALIAN OXTAIL STEW

Preparation time: 5 minutes
Cooking time: 12–15 hours
Serves 4–6

1.5kg (3lb 5oz) oxtail pieces

1 tbsp olive oil

75g (3oz) pancetta, cubed

150ml (5fl oz) dry white wine

1 red onion, peeled and thinly sliced

4 garlic cloves, peeled and thinly sliced

4 whole cloves

2 x 400g (14oz) tins chopped tomatoes

Sea salt and freshly ground black pepper

1 lemon (preferably unwaxed)

Rustic it may be. Simple, yes, but this gloriously rich stew is absolutely amazing. Perfect for the family and just as good for entertaining. Start with good-quality oxtail from a reputable butcher or supermarket and you won't go wrong.

Rinse the oxtail under cold running water and pat dry with kitchen paper. Warm the olive oil and pancetta in a large frying pan over a high heat. When hot, add the oxtail and cook for 10–15 minutes, turning occasionally, until all the pieces are browned.

Add the wine to the pan – be careful, it will bubble angrily at first. As soon as it calms down to a manageable level, pour into the slow cooker dish, then add the onion, garlic, cloves and tomatoes and mix well.

Cover with the lid and cook on low for 12–15 hours. Season to taste with salt and pepper. Using a very fine grater, zest the lemon over the oxtail, then serve immediately with green beans and plenty of creamy mash to soak up the juices.

COOKING CONVENTIONALLY?
Place everything in a casserole dish, cover with a tight-fitting lid or foil and cook in an oven preheated to 150°C (300°F), Gas mark 2 for 5–6 hours.

BARNSLEY HOTPOT

Preparation time: 10 minutes
Cooking time: 4-5 hours
Serves 4

4 Barnsley chops

25g (1oz) butter

3 large baking potatoes, peeled and cut into 5mm (¼in) slices

2 small onions, peeled and finely sliced

1 large carrot, peeled and sliced

2 garlic cloves, peeled and crushed

3 tbsp plain flour

1 tsp fresh thyme leaves

Sea salt and freshly ground black pepper

300ml (10fl oz) hot lamb or chicken stock

1 tbsp Worcestershire sauce

I'm a real fan of Lancashire hotpot. Here I'm using Barnsley chops, which are best described as a double lamb chop, cut across the loin with the bone running through the centre. They are now available in most decent supermarkets, or ask your butcher to prepare some for you.

Rinse the chops under cold running water and pat dry with kitchen paper. Butter the inside of the slow cooker dish liberally. Arrange the potato slices in an overlapping layer over the base of the dish. Top with the onions, carrot and garlic.

Place the flour and thyme leaves in a large freezer bag and season with salt and pepper. Add the lamb, seal the top and shake to coat in the flour. Tip the meat and any excess flour over the vegetables.

Mix the hot stock and Worcestershire sauce together in a jug, then pour the mixture over the meat. Cover with the lid and cook for 4-5 hours on low or until the meat is tender. Place the chops on warm plates and spoon over the vegetables to serve.

I ALSO LIKE...

using cubed lamb shoulder or neck instead of the chops in this recipe - you'll need about 500-600g (1lb 2oz-1lb 5oz).

BEEF STROGANOFF

I love beef stroganoff, but disappointingly the meat is often tough. In this recipe long slow cooking ensures that the beef is amazingly tender.

Cut the beef, across the grain, into thin strips. Mix the beef, onion, mushrooms, cornflour and brandy or water together in the slow cooker dish. Add the 4 tablespoons of water and season well with salt and pepper. Cover with the lid and cook on low for 8 hours or until the meat is tender.

Stir in the mustard, soured cream and the dill and season again to taste. Serve with freshly cooked rice or long thin pasta or noodles.

COOKING CONVENTIONALLY?
Preheat the oven to 180°C (350°F), Gas mark 4. Use an ovenproof casserole dish with a tight-fitting lid instead of a slow cooker and add 250ml (9fl oz) cold water in addition to the brandy or water. Cover and transfer to the oven. Cook for about 2 hours or until the beef is tender. Stir in the mustard, cream and dill and continue as above.

Preparation time: 15 minutes
Cooking time: 8 hours
Serves 4

500g (1lb 2oz) beef chuck or stewing steak

1 large onion, peeled and finely sliced

500g (1lb 2oz) cup mushrooms, cleaned and sliced

2 tbsp cornflour

2 tbsp brandy or water

4 tbsp cold water

Sea salt and freshly ground black pepper

2 tbsp Dijon mustard

150ml (5fl oz) soured cream

1 tbsp finely chopped fresh dill

CHINESE RED BRAISED BEEF

Brisket needs long, moist cooking to bring out its gloriously rich and almost sweet flavour. Cooking it in flavoured stock or sauce helps even more – which is why this recipe is so good!

Place all of the ingredients in the slow cooker dish and mix well.

Cover with the lid and cook on low for 8 hours, or for up to 12 hours, until the meat is meltingly tender.

Remove the meat from the slow cooker dish and carve into thick slices. Drizzle with the sauce and serve with noodles and steamed green vegetables.

I ALSO LIKE...
to make this recipe with a lighter vegetable stock in the summer months, or flavour it with summer herbs and white wine for a more European option.

Preparation time: 10 minutes
Cooking time: 8–12 hours
Serves 4–6

1.5kg (3lb 5oz) brisket joint

2 garlic cloves, peeled and left whole

150ml (5fl oz) light soy sauce

100ml (3½fl oz) dry sherry

1 tsp toasted sesame oil

1 tsp shredded fresh root ginger

½ tbsp Chinese five-spice powder

Pared rind of 1 orange

150ml (5fl oz) cold water

OX CHEEKS IN ALE WITH BARLEY AND HERB DUMPLINGS

Preparation time: 15 minutes
Cooking time: 12½ hours
Serves 4–6

2 ox cheeks (about 950g/2lb in total), diced into 3cm (1¼in) chunks

2 tbsp plain flour

Sea salt and freshly ground black pepper

4 tbsp olive oil

500ml (18fl oz) ale

2 celery sticks, trimmed and cut into 2–3cm (¾–1¼in) chunks

1 large carrot, peeled and cut into 2–3cm (¾–1¼in) chunks

1 leek, trimmed and cut into 2cm (¾in) chunks

25g (1oz) pearl barley

3 tbsp Worcestershire sauce

4 whole garlic cloves, peeled

2 fresh rosemary sprigs

FOR THE DUMPLINGS:

150g (5oz) self-raising flour, plus extra for dusting

75g (3oz) suet

2 tbsp roughly chopped fresh mixed herbs, such as parsley, mint and basil

About 100ml (3½fl oz) cold water

This rich and tasty stew is very economical to make. Check that your slow cooker dish can go in the oven before making the dumplings.

Pat the meat dry with kitchen paper. Place in a freezer bag with the flour and some salt and pepper. Seal the top and shake to coat the meat evenly.

Warm the olive oil in a large frying pan, and when hot add the meat and cook for 3–5 minutes until browned. Add 2 tablespoons of the ale to deglaze the pan, stirring to scrape up all the caramelised bits from the bottom. Tip into the slow cooker dish.

Add the celery, carrot, leek and barley to the slow cooker dish together with the Worcestershire sauce, garlic and rosemary and mix well. Cover with the lid and cook on low for 12 hours.

Stir well, then remove and discard the rosemary and season to taste with salt and pepper.

About an hour before you wish to eat, prepare the dumplings. Preheat your oven to 190°C (375°F), Gas mark 5. Using your hands, mix the flour, suet and herbs together in a large bowl. Season and add just enough water to bring the mixture together into a firm dough.

Roll the dough into 6–8 balls, dusting your hands with flour if the dough becomes sticky. Drop the dough balls onto the top of the beef mixture and place uncovered in the hot oven. Cook for 20–30 minutes or until golden and well risen.

COOKING CONVENTIONALLY?
Preheat the oven to 120°C (250°F), Gas mark ½. Brown the beef, place in a large ovenproof casserole dish with a tight-fitting lid and cook in the oven for 12 hours until piping hot and thick. Increase the temperature to 190°C (375°F), Gas mark 5, to cook the dumplings.

BEEF IN BLACK BEAN SAUCE

Preparation time: 20 minutes
Cooking time: 6¼ hours
Serves 6

750g (1lb 10oz) beef braising or stewing steak (chuck works well)

1 tbsp vegetable oil

1 tsp caster sugar

1 tbsp dark soy sauce

1 tbsp Chinese rice wine or dry sherry

1½ tsp cornflour

2 peppers (one green and one red if possible), deseeded and sliced into strips

4 spring onions, trimmed and cut into 3cm (1¼in) lengths

2 garlic cloves, peeled and finely chopped

About 3cm (1¼in) piece fresh root ginger, peeled and finely chopped

25g (1oz) Chinese fermented black beans, finely chopped, or 2 tbsp black bean sauce

This is a cracking recipe – although I say so myself! It's easy to make and the meat is gloriously tender. Buy the vacuum-packed Chinese fermented beans from Asian supermarkets, or buy the sauce in any supermarket.

Cut the beef, across the grain, into thin strips. Warm the vegetable oil in a large frying pan over a high heat. When hot, add the meat in batches and cook for 5–10 minutes or until browned all over. Transfer to the slow cooker dish, then add the sugar, soy sauce, rice wine or sherry and cornflour. Leave to marinate for 10 minutes.

Add the prepared vegetables and black beans or sauce to the slow cooker and mix well. Cover with the lid and cook on low for 6 hours or until the beef is tender.

Serve with freshly cooked rice or noodles.

I ALSO LIKE...
making this recipe with strips of lamb shoulder or neck.

ROASTS

AUBERGINE AND TOMATO BAKE

Preparation time: 10 minutes
Cooking time: 3 hours 10 minutes
Serves: 6

3 large aubergines

500g (1lb 2oz) jar good-quality tomato pasta sauce

3 tbsp extra virgin olive oil

A large handful of fresh basil leaves, plus extra to serve

Sea salt and freshly ground black pepper

75g (3oz) quartered black olives

100g (3½oz) grated mozzarella cheese

6 tbsp finely grated fresh Parmesan cheese

Aubergines and tomatoes are a fantastic pairing. Here they are used in an easy, layered bake, which benefits from its long slow cooking in terms of flavour and texture.

Using a sharp knife, trim the aubergines and slice them lengthways into thin slices no wider than a pound coin (about 3mm/⅛in).

Spread about 4 heaped tablespoons of pasta sauce over the base of the slow cooker dish, then top with a third of the aubergine slices and drizzle with some of the olive oil, add a layer of basil and season to taste with salt and pepper. Sprinkle over a third of the olives and a third of the cheeses. Repeat this process twice more, but do not add the final layer of cheese. Finish with the remaining pasta sauce, spreading it evenly over the aubergine slices. Cover with the lid and cook on high for 3 hours or on low for 6 hours until the aubergines are meltingly tender.

Uncover and sprinkle with the reserved mozzarella and Parmesan, then replace the lid and cook on high for a further 10 minutes or until melted. Serve with a dressed green salad.

I ALSO LIKE...
to add a couple of layers of lasagne sheets to this recipe to make a more substantial dish. See the lasagne recipe opposite for more guidance on quantities and how to do it.

WINTER VEGETABLE GRATIN

This comforting root vegetable gratin tastes fantastic and is just as good on its own as it is as an accompaniment.

Cut the garlic in half and rub over the inside of the slow cooker dish, pressing down firmly to release its juices. Using about a third of the butter, butter the inside of the slow cooker dish generously. Slice the vegetables into very thin 2–3mm (1/16–1/8in) slices (a mandolin or food processor with slicing attachment is the easiest way to do this).

Arrange the potato slices in an overlapping layer over the base of the dish. Season well with salt and pepper and dot with a little more of the butter. Sprinkle a third of the cheese and a third of the thyme leaves over the top. Repeat this process again using the swede slices first, and then the parsnips. Aim for the dish to be no more than half full.

In a large bowl, whisk the cream, milk and beaten eggs together, then pour the mixture over the vegetables (it should cover the vegetables completely). Cover with the lid and cook on high for 3–4 hours or until the vegetables are tender when tested with the tip of a knife.

Remove the dish from the slow cooker base and leave to rest for about 30 minutes.

If your slow cooker can be used under the grill (check the manufacturer's instructions) preheat the grill to its highest setting. Grill the top of the gratin for 3–5 minutes or until golden before serving. If not, just serve it as it is.

COOKING CONVENTIONALLY?
Layer the ingredients into a large ovenproof dish then cover with a double layer of buttered foil. Cook in an oven preheated to 160°C (325°F), Gas mark 3, for 1 hour before removing the foil and cooking for a further 30 minutes or until tender and golden.

Preparation time: 15–20 minutes
Cooking time: 3–4 hours, plus resting
Serves 6
Vegetarian

1 garlic clove

25g (1oz) softened butter

3 medium potatoes, peeled

½ small swede, peeled

1 parsnip, peeled

Sea salt and freshly ground black pepper

125g (4½oz) extra mature Cheddar cheese, grated

1 tsp fresh thyme leaves (lemon thyme tastes great in this!)

300ml (10fl oz) double cream

300ml (10fl oz) milk

4 medium eggs, beaten

WHOLE ROAST CHINESE CHICKEN WITH PLUMS

Preparation time: 15 minutes
Cooking time: 6 hours
Serves 4

1–1.5kg (2lb 4oz–3lb 5oz) free-range chicken

1 tbsp groundnut oil

1 tbsp Chinese five-spice powder

750g (1lb 10oz) just ripe plums (about 8), halved and stoned

75ml (2½ fl oz) dry fino sherry

150ml (5fl oz) vegetable stock

1 tbsp clear honey

Sea salt and freshly ground black pepper

Whole roast chicken isn't just for Sunday! Try this great dish – with Chinese five-spice and sherry giving the chicken a delicious Chinese flavour – on any day of the week. This is great served with freshly cooked noodles and steamed pak choi.

Pat the chicken dry with kitchen paper. Warm the groundnut oil in a large frying pan over a high heat. When hot, add the chicken and sear on all sides until golden brown. Allow to cool slightly, then rub with the five-spice powder.

Place the plums in the slow cooker dish together with the sherry and stock.

Cover with the lid and cook on low for 6 hours. Remove the chicken and set aside in a warm place covered in a tent of foil. Stir the honey into the plum sauce and season to taste with salt and pepper.

Carve the chicken into portions (it will be so tender that you may not need a knife, just a spoon and fork to divide it) and serve with plenty of sauce and plums spooned over.

TRY...
buying a bigger bird so that there is plenty left for a cold lunch the next day.

ROAST CHICKEN WITH CLEMENTINES

Preparation time: **10 minutes**
Cooking time: **6½ hours**
Serves **4**

1–1.5kg (2lb 4oz–3lb 5oz) whole free-range chicken

2 tbsp olive oil

4 clementines

1 onion, peeled and very finely sliced

2 large carrots, peeled and diced

2 tbsp clear honey

150ml (5fl oz) dry white wine

25g (1oz) butter, cut into cubes

Sea salt and freshly ground black pepper

2 tbsp chopped fresh flat-leaf parsley

This simple roast chicken recipe works wonders at any time of the year.

Wash the chicken inside and out and pat dry with kitchen paper. Warm the olive oil in a large frying pan over a high heat. When hot, add the chicken and cook for 10 minutes, turning frequently until golden all over. Set aside.

Wash and dry the clementines. Place two of them, skin on, inside the cavity of the chicken. Roughly chop the remaining clementines, again with the skin on, and place them in the slow cooker dish together with the onion, carrots, honey and wine and mix together well.

Place the chicken on the bed of fruit and vegetables and pour over any juices that may have gathered in the pan. Cover with the lid and cook on low for 6 hours or until the chicken is tender and there is no pink meat.

Remove the chicken from the slow cooker, place on a board and leave to rest for 10–15 minutes.

Meanwhile, skim off any excess fat from the surface of the cooking liquid, then strain the sauce through a sieve into a saucepan. Bring to the boil over a high heat and bubble vigorously for 5–10 minutes or until reduced by about one-third. Reduce the heat and slowly whisk in the butter, piece by piece. Season to taste with salt and pepper and add the parsley. Carve the chicken and serve with the sauce.

I ALSO LIKE...
to use other citrus fruits – lemons, blood oranges and tangerines all work well.

ROAST CHICKEN WITH SAFFRON AND MOROCCAN VEGETABLES

The slow cooker makes easy work of a roast chicken and ensures wonderfully moist meat. Harissa is a spicy Moroccan chilli paste and is available from all good supermarkets.

Wash the chicken inside and out and pat dry with kitchen paper. Cut the orange in half and push one of the pieces and one of the red onions into the cavity of the chicken.

Warm the juice from the other orange half in a small saucepan over a medium heat for 1 minute. Remove from the heat and add the saffron strands. Leave to stand for 5–10 minutes.

Cut the remaining onion into large chunks and place in the slow cooker dish together with the remaining vegetables. Mix in the harissa paste and season with salt and pepper. Place the chicken on the bed of vegetables.

Using a pastry brush or your fingers, 'paint' the saffron-infused orange juice over the chicken (it will colour it a beautiful yellow). Cover with the lid and cook on low for 6 hours or until the chicken is tender and there is no pink meat.

Remove the chicken from the slow cooker, place on a board and leave to rest for 10–15 minutes. Skim off any excess fat from the surface of the cooking liquid. Stir the coriander and seasoning to taste into the vegetables and serve immediately.

Preparation time: 15 minutes
Cooking time: 6 hours
Serves **4**

1–1.5kg (2lb 4oz–3lb 5oz) whole free-range chicken

1 orange

2 red onions, peeled

2 large pinches of saffron strands

2 celery sticks, trimmed and cut into large chunks

1 large carrot, peeled and cut into large chunks

1 large courgette, trimmed and cut into large chunks

2 tsp harissa paste, or to taste

Sea salt and freshly ground black pepper

2 tbsp chopped fresh coriander

TURKEY BALLOTINE WITH CHESTNUTS AND PORT

Preparation time: 25 minutes, plus chilling
Cooking time: 6 ¼ hours, plus preheating
Serves 2

25g (1oz) butter, chilled and diced

75g (3oz) cooked and peeled chestnuts, finely chopped

1 shallot, peeled and finely chopped

Sea salt and freshly ground black pepper

2 tbsp port

1 large turkey leg or thigh joint, about 800g (1lb 12oz)

125g (4½oz) good-quality sausage meat

2 tbsp chopped fresh flat-leaf parsley

100ml (3½fl oz) dry white wine

1 bay leaf

2 tbsp double cream

This recipe works really well in the slow cooker and stays wonderfully moist. It is delicious served with roast parsnips and baby carrots.

Melt half of the butter in a frying pan over a medium heat. Add the chestnuts and shallot and sauté for about 5 minutes or until softened and just starting to colour. Season well with salt and pepper, then add the port and cook for a minute or until reduced. Leave to cool.

Using a sharp knife, cut the turkey leg lengthways down to the bone, using short delicate strokes to cut the meat away from the bone and being careful not to puncture the skin. Remove the bone and set aside, covered, in the fridge for later. Open the leg meat out like a book and lay it skin side down on a board. Use the same light strokes to remove any tough cartilage or smaller bones.

Place the sausage meat in a bowl together with the cooled chestnut mixture and the parsley. Mix well and season to taste. Spread the mixture onto the turkey meat, then roll the meat up firmly like a Swiss roll. Season the skin with salt and pepper. Wrap the turkey roll very tightly in several layers of foil and twist the ends tightly like a sweet to seal. Place in the fridge for at least 12 hours or for up to 24 hours.

To cook, cover the base of the slow cooker with about 5mm (¼in) cold water and add the wine. Cover with the lid and preheat the slow cooker on high for 30 minutes.

Add the bay leaf to the hot mixture in the slow cooker. Reduce the temperature to low and place the foil parcel and the reserved turkey bone (if it will fit) in the slow cooker dish. Cover with the lid and cook on low for 6 hours, turning the parcel over halfway through, until tender and there is no more pink meat.

Carefully remove the parcel from the slow cooker with tongs, place on a board and leave to stand for 10–15 minutes before unwrapping and cutting into thick slices.

To make a simple gravy, discard the bone, then strain the juices from the parcel and the slow cooker dish through a sieve into a small saucepan. Bring to the boil over a high heat and boil rapidly for 2 minutes. Slowly whisk in the cream. Serve the turkey in slices with the gravy spooned over, and all the usual festive veg and trimmings.

ROAST TURKEY LEG WITH RED WINE SAUCE

Preparation time: 20 minutes
Cooking time: 4¾–6¾ hours
Serves 4

2 turkey drumsticks

50g (2oz) plain flour

Sea salt and freshly ground black pepper

25g (1oz) butter

1 tbsp olive oil

12 baby shallots, peeled

200g (7oz) smoked streaky bacon, diced

250ml (9fl oz) red wine

2 bay leaves, broken

2 fresh thyme sprigs

2 celery sticks, trimmed and diced

4 garlic cloves, peeled and roughly chopped

250ml (9fl oz) chicken stock or water

2 tbsp concentrated tomato purée

Coq au vin has always been a favourite of mine, but I often use turkey instead of chicken. It's so economical and cooks brilliantly in the slow cooker.

Place the turkey in a large freezer bag with the flour and some salt and pepper. Seal the top and shake the bag to coat the meat in the flour.

Warm a large frying pan over a high heat, and when hot add the butter and olive oil. When the butter has melted, add the shallots and fry for 5–10 minutes or until golden. Transfer them to the slow cooker dish with a slotted spoon.

Return the pan to the heat, add the bacon and cook for 3–5 minutes or until golden. Add them to the shallots in the slow cooker. Finally brown the turkey legs in the same pan for 5–10 minutes or until golden all over. Transfer to the slow cooker.

Add the wine to the now empty frying pan and stir well to scrape up any bits from the bottom of the pan. Pour over the turkey and surround with the herbs, celery, garlic, stock and tomato purée. Cover with the lid and cook on low for 4–6 hours or until the turkey is tender and there is no pink meat.

Remove the meat from the slow cooker, place on a plate and set aside. Skim off any excess fat from the surface of the cooking liquid and strain the liquid through a large sieve into a large saucepan. Set the vegetables aside with the turkey.

Bring the sauce to the boil over a high heat and cook for 5–10 minutes or until reduced by about one-third, then season to taste with salt and pepper. When the turkey is just cool enough to handle, remove the meat from the bones and discard any skin. Mix the meat, reserved vegetables and bacon into the sauce. Serve with mash and seasonal green vegetables.

DUCK WITH STICKY POMEGRANATE AND ORANGE SAUCE

This wonderful dish is great served with couscous.

Remove the giblets and any excess fat from the inside of the bird. Prick the skin all over with the tip of a sharp knife, then place the duck in a clean kitchen sink and pour a kettle full of boiling water over the bird (this will help to remove some of the excess fat). Repeat this process again.

Cut one of the oranges in half and use it to fill the cavity of the bird together with the whole onion and thyme. Place the duck, breast side down, in the slow cooker dish, cover with the lid and cook on low for 1 hour.

Carefully pour the fat away into a bowl (don't discard it, though – it's great for crispy roast potatoes). Cover with the lid again and continue cooking the duck for a further hour, then pour the fat off a second time. Turn the bird over, so it is breast side up.

Finely grate the zest from the remaining 2 oranges over the duck, then pour over the orange juice and half of the pomegranate juice. Cover with the lid again and increase the temperature to high. Cook for 1–2 hours or until tender and the juices run clear when tested with the tip of a knife (or see tip below).

Carefully lift the bird out of the slow cooker, draining off any juices that may have gathered in the cavity and place on a plate or board. Cover with a tent of foil and leave to rest in a warm place for about 15 minutes.

Skim off the excess fat in the slow cooker dish, leaving only the meaty cooking juices behind. Pour these juices into a small saucepan together with the remaining pomegranate juice. Season to taste with salt and pepper and bring to the boil over a high heat. Boil for 5–10 minutes or until reduced and thickened slightly. Taste and add more seasoning if necessary, then carve the duck and serve with the sticky sauce spooned over the top.

I ALSO LIKE...
to test poultry and duck with a meat thermometer before serving – poke the clean thermometer into the thickest part of the meat, avoiding the bones as these hold the heat. The core temperature should be at least 75°C (167°F).

Preparation time: 5 minutes
Cooking time: 3¼–4¼ hours
Serves 4–6

2–2.5kg (4lb 8oz–5lb 8oz) free-range duck

3 large oranges

1 large onion, peeled

3 fresh thyme sprigs

250ml (9fl oz) pomegranate juice

Sea salt and freshly ground black pepper

GAMMON WITH CUMBERLAND AND ORANGE SAUCE

Preparation time: 10 minutes
Cooking time: 6-8 hours
Serves 6

1.5kg (3lb 5oz) gammon joint (check this will fit your slow cooker dish)

1 red onion, peeled and thinly sliced

1 orange

1 lemon (preferably unwaxed)

6 tbsp good-quality redcurrant jelly

4 tbsp port

1 tsp mustard powder

1 tsp ground ginger

Sea salt and freshly ground black pepper

Gammon with Cumberland sauce and mashed potatoes reminds me of Boxing Day with all the family. It is a fabulous combination of flavours and the slow cooker makes easy work of the cooking, as it's an all-in-one dish.

Wash the gammon under cold running water and pat dry with kitchen paper. Place the onion in the slow cooker dish and top with the gammon, fat side up.

Using a potato peeler, thinly pare off the zest from the orange and lemon, then using a sharp knife cut the zest into very thin strips. Place the strips in a small bowl and pour over enough boiling water to cover. Leave to stand for 5 minutes to draw out the bitter-tasting oils. Drain well.

Remove the segments from the orange over a bowl to catch the juice and scatter these with any juice around the gammon. Add the blanched zests, the juice of half a lemon, the redcurrant jelly, port, mustard powder and ginger to the slow cooker. Cover with the lid and cook on low for 6-8 hours or until the meat is tender.

Remove the gammon from the slow cooker, place on a plate or board and leave to rest under a tent of foil for 10 minutes.

Meanwhile, skim off any excess fat from the surface of the cooking liquid. Season the remaining sauce to taste and mix well to ensure that there are no lumps of mustard powder remaining. Serve the gammon in slices with the sauce spooned over.

ITALIAN MILK-FED PORK

Preparation time: 15 minutes
Cooking time: 6¼–8¼ hours
Serves 4

2kg (4lb 7oz) pork loin roast, on the bone

---

2 tbsp olive oil

50g (2oz) butter

---

1 onion, peeled and sliced

---

2 celery sticks, trimmed and diced

1–1.5 litres (1¾–2½ pints) whole milk

---

4 bay leaves

---

4 sage leaves

Pared zest of 1 orange

---

1 cinnamon stick

---

2 garlic cloves, peeled

Cooking pork in milk has been done for years in Italy. It gives the meat a wonderful mild flavour and amazing succulence.

Wash the pork under cold running water and pat dry with kitchen paper. Warm a large frying pan over a high heat. When hot add the olive oil and butter, and when melted and bubbling add the meat and cook for 5-10 minutes or until browned all over.

Place the onion and celery in the slow cooker dish and spread out to cover the base. Top with the meat. Deglaze the pan with a little of the milk, stirring to scrape up any crusty bits from the bottom of the pan.

Pour the contents of the pan into the slow cooker. Pour in enough milk to cover the meat, then add the herbs, orange zest, cinnamon and garlic. Cover with the lid and cook for 6-8 hours, turning once, until the pork is cooked and the sauce is curdled (don't worry – it really is supposed to be like that!).

Remove and discard the orange rind, herbs and spices. Remove the pork from the slow cooker and place on a board. Cut the pork into thin slices and arrange on serving plates, then spoon over the curd sauce. Serve with steamed seasonal green vegetables.

I ALSO LIKE...
to cook pork chops on the bone in the same way. Cook for a maximum of 4 hours, using only enough milk to cover the meat.

ALL-IN-ONE PORK AND APPLE SAUCE

An absolute favourite in our house – and so easy!

Rinse the joint under cold running water and pat dry with kitchen paper. Place the apples in the slow cooker dish. Add the lemon zest and juice and stir well to coat the apple pieces. Add the sugar, thyme, bay leaves and water and mix well. Season to taste.

Place the meat, fat side up, on the apple mixture (it's important that the meat covers the apples completely to prevent them from turning brown). Cover with the lid and cook on low for 8–10 hours.

If you like crackling, preheat your grill to its highest setting. Place the cooked pork under the grill for about 5 minutes or until golden and bubbling. Leave to stand for 5 minutes before carving into thick slices and serve with the apple sauce.

COOKING CONVENTIONALLY?
Preheat the oven to 150°C (300°F), Gas mark 2. Place the pork in a roasting tin just large enough to accommodate it in a single layer and bake in the oven for 5 hours. Increase the temperature to 220°C (425°F), Gas mark 7, for the final 15–20 minutes for the crackling.

Preparation time: 15 minutes
Cooking time: 8–10 hours
Serves 6–8

2kg (4lb 7oz) pork belly (check that it fits the slow cooker – it needs to be just larger than the base of the dish)

3 Bramley apples, peeled, cored and diced

Finely grated zest and juice of 1 lemon (preferably unwaxed)

2 tsp caster sugar

1 fresh thyme sprig

2 bay leaves, broken

100ml (3½fl oz) cold water

Sea salt and freshly ground black pepper

SLOW-ROASTED PORK BELLY WITH LENTILS AND TARRAGON

Preparation time: 10 minutes
Cooking time: 6½ hours
Serves 4–6

1–1.5kg (2lb 4oz–3lb 5oz) pork belly joint (the joint needs to fit into your slow cooker flat, without being folded or rolled)

Sea salt and freshly ground black pepper

4 celery sticks, trimmed and cut into diagonal slices

2 large red onions, peeled and cut into thin wedges

4 garlic cloves, peeled and left whole

3 fresh tarragon sprigs

200g (7oz) Puy lentils

½ bottle red wine

Tarragon is an ideal accompaniment to the pork and, rather than dominate, it gives the dish a wonderfully rounded flavour.

Unroll the pork belly if you need to so that you have a flat rectangular piece of meat and dry thoroughly with kitchen paper. If the skin on the belly has not been scored, then use a very sharp knife to score it in even lines every centimetre or so. Rub with 1 tablespoon of salt, massaging it well into every scored cut, then leave in the fridge until needed.

Place the celery, onions, garlic, 2 sprigs of the tarragon, the lentils and the wine in the slow cooker dish and mix well. Do not season. Place the pork, skin side up, in a single layer on top of the vegetables. Cover with the lid and cook on low for 6 hours or until the vegetables are soft.

Preheat the grill to its highest setting. If your slow cooker dish is happy under the grill (check the manufacturer's instructions), grill the pork still in the slow cooker dish for 5–10 minutes or until well browned, puffed up and crispy. Alternatively, transfer the pork from the slow cooker dish to a grill tray and cook the pork under the grill. Remove the grilled pork and place on a wooden board or warm serving plate.

Roughly chop the reserved tarragon and mix into the lentils. Season to taste. Serve with slices of pork on top and the cooking juices drizzled over.

ROLLED ROAST PORK WITH SPICED PEAR CHUTNEY

Preparation time: **25 minutes**
Cooking time: **6–8 hours**
Serves **8**

2kg (4lb 7oz) boned and rolled pork shoulder

1 x 400g (14oz) tin pear quarters in natural juice

200ml (7fl oz) dry cider or apple juice

3 tbsp golden caster sugar

1 cinnamon stick

¼ tsp crushed dried chillies

A pinch of freshly grated nutmeg

Sea salt and freshly ground black pepper

FOR THE SPICE PASTE:

2 tsp fennel seeds

1 tsp coriander seeds

¼ tsp black peppercorns

1 tsp dried chilli flakes, or to taste

3 tsp sea salt

4 garlic cloves, peeled and crushed

Finely grated zest and juice of 1 lemon (preferably unwaxed)

Pork and pears are a classic combination. Here, I have used tinned pears as fresh ones can turn brown during slow cooking – it also makes it a great store-cupboard recipe.

Remove the strings from the pork and unroll it. Lay it out flat on a board, fat side upper-most. Using a very sharp knife, score the skin deeply at 1cm (½in) intervals (or ask your butcher to do this for you). Turn the meat over.

To make the spice paste, place the fennel, coriander, peppercorns, chilli flakes, salt, garlic and lemon zest and juice in a food processor or use a mortar and blitz or pound to make a thick paste.

Smother the upper side of the meat with two-thirds of the paste and place 3–4 pieces of pear along the left-hand end of the meat. Re-roll the pork from the left-hand side like a Swiss roll, so that the pear quarters are in the centre. Re-tie the meat with fresh kitchen string at 2cm (¾in) intervals and smooth the remaining paste over the outside of the meat.

Dice the remaining pears and add them to the slow cooker dish together with their juice, the cider or apple juice, the sugar, cinnamon, chillies and nutmeg. Mix well, then place the meat on top. Cover with the lid and cook on low for 6–8 hours or until the meat is tender.

If you like crackling, preheat your grill to its highest setting. Place the pork under the grill for about 5 minutes or until golden and bubbling. Leave to stand for 5 minutes before carving into thick slices. Season the pear chutney to taste with salt and pepper and serve with the pork.

I ALSO LIKE...
making sure I've cooked too much so there's plenty left over for pork sandwiches the next day!

SHOULDER OF PORK WITH FENNEL AND PEARS

Shoulder of pork can be a little fatty but slow cooking allows the fat to melt into the meat, giving it loads of extra flavour and succulence. You can also use pork chops (cook on high for 3 hours).

Dry the surface of the pork with kitchen paper. Roughly crush the fennel seeds and salt together in a mortar with a pestle to release some of their flavour. Spread the mustard over the fat on the top of the meat and press the fennel salt on top of the mustard layer. Place the meat in the slow cooker dish.

Pour the cider around the meat, being careful not to splash the fennel topping, then place the pears around the meat.

Cover with the lid and cook on low for 8–9 hours. Remove the pork from the slow cooker dish and carve into thick slices. Serve with some pear pieces and cooking juices spooned over, accompanied by creamy mash and freshly cooked seasonal vegetables.

Preparation time: 10 minutes
Cooking time: 8–9 hours
Serves 4–6

1.2kg (2lb 12oz) rolled shoulder of pork (bone removed)

2 tbsp fennel seeds

1 tsp sea salt

3 tbsp Dijon mustard

150ml (5fl oz) dry perry or cider

2 pears, peeled, cored and cut into quarters

HOISIN PORK ROAST

This simple recipe tastes great and is perfect for all the family. Serve with Chinese pancakes, rice or noodles.

Wash the meat under cold running water and pat dry with kitchen paper. Mix the hoisin sauce, garlic, ginger, chilli flakes, soy sauce, sesame oil and cornflour together in the slow cooker dish. Add the pork and roll it in the mixture until coated. Cover with the lid and cook on low for 6–8 hours.

Remove the meat from the slow cooker, place on a platter or board and leave to rest under a tent of foil for 10 minutes.

Skim off any excess fat from the surface of the cooking liquid. Slice the pork and arrange on a serving platter. Sprinkle the spring onions and coriander over the top and serve the hot sauce on the side.

I ALSO LIKE...
to use pork belly for this recipe.

Preparation time: 5 minutes
Cooking time: 6–8 hours
Serves 6

1.5 kg (3lb 5oz) boneless pork shoulder joint

175g (6oz) hoisin sauce

2 garlic cloves, peeled and crushed

1 tbsp grated fresh root ginger

¼ tsp dried chilli flakes

1 tbsp dark soy sauce

2 tsp roasted sesame oil

2 tsp cornflour

2 spring onions, trimmed and finely shredded

4 tbsp roughly chopped fresh coriander

ROLLED LAMB WITH CAPERS AND ANCHOVIES

Preparation time: 15 minutes
Cooking time: 6–8 hours
Serves 4

1–1.5kg (2lb 4oz–3lb 5oz) rolled shoulder of lamb, bone removed

2 tbsp baby capers in brine, rinsed and drained

2 garlic cloves, peeled

1 x 50g (2oz) tin anchovy fillets in olive oil, drained

2 fresh lemon thyme sprigs, leaves only

2 tbsp cold water

Lamb and anchovies are a surprising but brilliant team. The saltiness of the fish really lifts the flavour of the meat.

Remove the strings from the lamb and unroll. Place it fat side down on a board.

Place the capers, garlic, anchovies and thyme leaves into a mini processor or use a pestle and mortar and blitz or pound to make a coarse paste. Spread the paste over the meat side of the lamb. Re-roll the lamb to form its original shape and tie with kitchen string at 2cm (¾in) intervals.

Place the meat in the slow cooker dish and drizzle over the water. Cover with the lid and cook on low for 6–8 hours or until tender.

Remove the lamb from the slow cooker, place on a board and leave to rest for 10 minutes before carving into thick slices, discarding the string. Serve with roasted new potatoes and dollops of Greek yoghurt.

I ALSO LIKE...
to omit the anchovies in this recipe when any fish-hating friends come for supper! The recipe still tastes great; just add 2 tablespoons of olive oil to the paste when you make it.

ROLLED BREAST OF LAMB WITH REDCURRANT AND ROSEMARY

Preparation time: 15 minutes

Cooking time: 4–6 hours

Serves 4

2 rolled breasts of lamb, about 400g (14oz) each

175g (6oz) redcurrant jelly

3 fresh rosemary sprigs, roughly chopped

2 garlic cloves, peeled and crushed

2 shallots, peeled and finely chopped

3 tbsp natural breadcrumbs

Sea salt and freshly ground black pepper

2 red onions, peeled and finely sliced

100ml (3½fl oz) red wine or water

It's great to see lamb breast readily available in supermarkets again. It's a fabulously flavoursome cut, perfect for slow cooking.

Snip the string from the lamb and unravel, laying the pieces out flat on a board.

Mix the redcurrant jelly, rosemary, garlic, shallots and breadcrumbs together in a bowl. Season to taste. Spread the redcurrant mixture over the lamb, then top with the other piece of meat. Roll the whole lot up together like a Swiss roll into one cylindrical shape and re-tie with kitchen string.

Place the red onions in the slow cooker dish to make a bed for the meat. Season to taste. Top with the lamb and pour over the wine or water together with any remaining redcurrant stuffing that may have oozed out during rolling. Cover with the lid and cook on low for 4–6 hours or until tender.

Remove the meat from the slow cooker, place on a plate or board and leave to rest for about 5 minutes before carving into 4 thick slices.

COOKING CONVENTIONALLY?

Cook in a roasting tin in an oven preheated to 160°C (325°F), Gas mark 3, for about 1 hour or until tender.

TOMATO-SIMMERED LAMB SHANKS

The rich, sweet meat on lamb shanks works wonderfully with the sweetness and slight acidity of the tomato sauce in this recipe. If shanks aren't available try using lamb shoulder instead.

Mix the onion, garlic, rosemary, tomatoes and wine together in the slow cooker dish. Season well with salt and pepper.

Fit the shanks in a snug single layer on top and push them down into the tomato mixture so that they are immersed in the sauce.

Cover with the lid and cook on low for 8–9 hours. The meat will have produced lots of fat during cooking, so spoon off as much of this from the surface of the stew as possible and discard. Serve the shanks with couscous or mash and a large green salad.

COOKING CONVENTIONALLY?
Place in a casserole dish, cover with a tight-fitting lid or foil and cook in an oven preheated to 170°C (325°F), Gas mark 3 for 4–6 hours.

Preparation time: 5 minutes
Cooking time: 8–9 hours
Serves 4

---

1 red onion, peeled, halved and finely sliced

---

2 garlic cloves, peeled and finely sliced

---

1 large fresh rosemary sprig

---

2 x 400g (14oz) tins chopped tomatoes

100ml (3½fl oz) red wine

Sea salt and freshly ground black pepper

---

4 lamb shanks, about 350g (12oz) each

ROLLED SHOULDER OF LAMB WITH CUMIN AND HARISSA

Preparation time: 15 minutes
Cooking time: 4 hours
Serves 4

800g (1lb 12oz) boneless lamb shoulder joint

1–2 tsp harissa paste, to taste

1 tsp cumin seeds

1 tbsp olive oil

500g (1lb 2oz) new potatoes, washed

150g (5oz) Greek yogurt

A large pinch of ground cumin

This is so easy to make and so tasty. If you like your food spicy, then add more harissa. This dish is great served with wilted spinach.

If the lamb is tied with string snip them with scissors and remove. Unroll the meat to give one flat piece, fat side down. Rub the harissa paste over the upper side of the meat and sprinkle with the cumin seeds. Roll the meat back up tightly and, using cooking string, tie the meat 3–4 times along the joint to stop it from springing open.

Warm the olive oil in a frying pan over a high heat. When hot, add the lamb and cook for about 5–10 minutes until the meat is browned all over.

Place the lamb in the slow cooker dish and pile the potatoes in around it. Cover with the lid and cook on low for 4 hours.

Spoon the yogurt into a serving dish and sprinkle with ground cumin. Serve the lamb in thick slices with the potatoes on the side and the fragrant yogurt to spoon over.

I ALSO LIKE...
using rolled pork shoulder or leg instead.

LAMB WITH 40 CLOVES OF GARLIC

Preparation time: 5 minutes
Cooking time: 16 hours
Serves 4-6

1.5–2kg (3lb 5oz–4lb 7oz) shoulder of lamb, bone in (depending on the size of your slow cooker dish – you want the lamb to completely cover the base)

1 tsp paprika

1 tsp fennel seeds (optional)

1 large onion, peeled and finely sliced

40 garlic cloves (about 3–5 whole heads), peeled

Sea salt and freshly ground black pepper

I've seen many recipes over the years for chicken with 40 cloves, but thought I would give lamb a try instead. I'm pleased to report that it's amazing and perfect for the slow cooker!

Wash the lamb under cold running water and pat dry with kitchen paper. Rub the meat with the paprika and fennel.

Place the onion in the slow cooker dish, spreading it evenly over the base. Press each garlic clove with your thumb or the back of a knife to just break the surface of each one, but not crush them, and scatter over the onion.

Position the meat over the garlic, fat side up. Cover with the lid and cook on low for 16 hours or until falling off the bone.

Remove the meat from the slow cooker and place on a plate or board. Use 2 forks to shred the meat.

Skim off any excess fat from the surface of the cooking juices. Season to taste with salt and pepper, then serve the meat with the gorgeous cooking juices spooned over.

I ALSO LIKE...
making this recipe with a large bone-in pork roast.

BEEF IN MISO

This Japanese-inspired dish is really easy to make and is wonderfully tasty. After cooking you're left with gorgeously tender meat and a rich, dark miso broth.

Wash the beef under cold running water and pat dry with kitchen paper. Place the shiitake mushrooms in a bowl and pour over enough boiling water to cover. Leave for 5 minutes or until soft. Remove the mushrooms from the water, reserving the flavoured water for later, and slice the mushrooms thickly.

Stir the miso paste into the mushroom-soaking liquid and add this mixture to the slow cooker dish together with the mushrooms and celery. Top with the meat and pour over enough water to come halfway up the meat. Cover with the lid and cook on low for 6 hours or until tender.

Stir in the soya beans and continue cooking, uncovered, for 15–20 minutes or until the beans are tender.

Remove the beef from the slow cooker and cut into wafer-thin slices. Season the 'broth' with more miso to taste. Divide the cooked noodles between six shallow bowls and top with some slices of meat. Ladle over the broth and sprinkle the coriander leaves over to serve.

COOKING CONVENTIONALLY?
Cook in an ovenproof casserole dish with a tight-fitting lid in an oven preheated to 150°C (300°F), Gas mark 2, for 3 hours or until tender.

Preparation time: 10 minutes
Cooking time: 6½ hours
Serves 6

2kg (4lb 7oz) beef silverside or topside

10 whole dried shiitake mushrooms

2 tbsp miso paste, plus extra to taste

2 celery sticks, trimmed and diced

100g (3½oz) frozen soya beans, defrosted

Cooked rice noodles, about 50–60g (2–2½oz) per person

Fresh coriander leaves, for sprinkling

BLACK VELVET CELEBRATION 'PIES'

Preparation time: 25 minutes
Cooking time: 10½–15½ hours
Serves 8

1.5kg (3lb 5oz) diced braising steak

3 tbsp plain flour, plus extra for dusting

1 tsp English mustard powder

3 tbsp olive oil

18 baby shallots, peeled

300g (10oz) baby button mushrooms, cleaned and trimmed

1 large carrot, peeled and finely diced

1 large celery stick, trimmed and finely diced

2 tbsp concentrated tomato purée

300ml (10fl oz) Guinness

250ml (9fl oz) brut dry champagne or dry sparkling wine

500g (1lb 2oz) puff pastry

2 tbsp milk, for glazing

75g (3oz) Irish blue cheese, cut into cubes

Sea salt and freshly ground black pepper

These individual pies are a bit of a cheat really as you cook the pastry separately, but they taste great and are perfect when feeding a crowd.

Pat the diced beef dry with kitchen paper and place in a large freezer bag together with the flour and mustard powder. Seal the top and shake well to coat the meat.

Warm a third of the olive oil in a large frying pan over a high heat. When hot, add the beef, in batches if necessary, and cook until well browned all over. Place in the slow cooker dish.

Return the pan to the heat and add another third of the oil and the shallots. Cook for about 5 minutes or until evenly browned. Add to the slow cooker, then repeat the process with the rest of the oil and the mushrooms, cooking for 5 minutes or until no more liquid remains in the pan.

Mix the vegetables (including the cooked mushrooms), tomato purée, Guinness and champagne or wine into the meat mixture. Cover with the lid and cook on low for 10–15 hours or until rich and tender.

About half an hour before the beef is ready or you wish to eat, preheat the oven to 190°C (375°F), Gas mark 5. Roll out the pastry on a well-floured surface until it is about 5mm (¼in) thick. Using a round cutter, stamp out 6 circles each about 10cm (4in) across. Using the tip of a sharp knife, score the tops with a criss-cross pattern.

Place the pastry circles on a non-stick baking tray. Brush with a little milk to glaze and cook in the oven for 10–15 minutes or until golden and risen.

Five minutes before serving, mix the blue cheese into the meat mixture and leave it to melt into the sauce. Season to taste with salt and pepper. Spoon the meat onto serving plates and top each one with a hot pastry circle. Serve with buttered green veggies and some colcannon.

I ALSO LIKE...

to roll, cut and cook the pastry circles in advance, and store in an airtight container for up to three days. Reheat for about 3–5 minutes in an oven preheated to 190°C (375°F), Gas mark 5, when ready to eat.

ITALIAN POT-ROAST BEEF

Preparation time: 15 minutes
Cooking time: 6¼–8¼ hours
Serves 8

1–2kg (2lb 4oz–4lb 7oz) beef chuck roast or pot-roast joint

4 garlic cloves, peeled and halved lengthways

8 fresh rosemary sprigs

Sea salt and freshly ground black pepper

1 tbsp olive oil

1 x 400g (14oz) tin chopped tomatoes

2 tbsp concentrated tomato purée

1 large red onion, peeled and cut into 8 wedges

200ml (7fl oz) red wine

This classic combination of flavours works so well with slow-cooked beef dishes.

Using a small sharp knife, cut 8 deep slits in the beef. Stuff the slits with the garlic and rosemary and season the meat generously with salt and pepper.

Warm the olive oil in a large frying pan over a high heat. When hot, add the meat and cook for 5–10 minutes or until browned on all sides.

Place the tomatoes, tomato purée and onion in the slow cooker dish and mix well. Top with the seared beef.

Return the pan to the heat and add the red wine, stirring continuously to scrape up any bits from the bottom of the pan. Pour the contents of the pan over the meat. Cover with the lid and cook on low for 6–8 hours or until tender.

Remove the beef from the slow cooker, place on a board and leave to rest for 5–10 minutes.

Skim off any excess fat from the surface of the cooking liquid. Cut the beef into wafer-thin slices and serve with the sauce and vegetables spooned over.

COOKING CONVENTIONALLY?
Preheat the oven to 180°C (350°F), Gas mark 4. Brown the beef in a large ovenproof casserole dish on the hob, then add the remaining ingredients, cover with a tight-fitting lid and cook in the oven for 3 hours or until tender.

BRISKET COOKED IN COFFEE

This recipe might sound a bit weird, but have faith! I discovered several American recipes that involved slow cooking beef in coffee and thought I really must give it a go – the resulting sauce is rich and tasty, with a wonderful flavour. Definitely worth a try!

Rinse the meat under cold running water and pat dry with kitchen paper. Place the vegetables in the slow cooker dish together with the thyme, then mix in the tomato purée. Top with the meat and season with salt and pepper. Pour the coffee over the top. Cover with the lid and cook on low for 6–8 hours.

Remove the meat from the slow cooker, place on a board and leave to rest under a tent of foil for 5–10 minutes.

Pour the sauce into a saucepan and bring to the boil over a high heat. Boil for about 5–10 minutes or until reduced and starting to thicken. Cut the meat into wafer-thin slices and drizzle with the sauce.

FAB FOR THE FREEZER
Leave to cool completely and then freeze for up to three months. Defrost thoroughly, then carve the meat and gently reheat in the sauce on the hob (never in the slow cooker).

Preparation time: **10 minutes**
Cooking time: **6¼–8¼ hours**
Serves **6**

1.3kg (2lb 13oz) rolled brisket joint

2 carrots, peeled and diced

2 celery sticks, peeled and diced

1 large onion, peeled and diced

2 fresh thyme sprigs

2 tbsp concentrated tomato purée

Sea salt and freshly ground black pepper

250ml (9fl oz) strong black coffee

MANZO ARROSTO (STUFFED ROLLED BEEF)

Preparation time: 20 minutes
Cooking time: 5–6 hours
Serves 6

1.3kg (2lb 13oz) rolled brisket joint

75g (3oz) baby spinach leaves

FOR THE FILLING:

50g (2oz) lean minced beef

25g (1oz) minced pork (or use all beef if you'd rather)

1 garlic clove, peeled and crushed

1 tbsp roughly chopped fresh parsley leaves

4 tsp finely grated fresh Parmesan cheese

2 tbsp fresh breadcrumbs

1 medium egg, beaten

¼ tsp sea salt

½ tbsp olive oil

FOR THE SAUCE:

4 tbsp good-quality olive oil

3 garlic cloves, peeled and roughly chopped

4 fresh bay leaves

200ml (7fl oz) white wine

2 tsp sea salt

2 x 400g (14oz) tins whole plum tomatoes

4 tbsp concentrated tomato purée

6 tbsp roughly chopped fresh flat-leaf parsley leaves and some tender stalks

There are all sorts of versions and regional Italian variations of this recipe. This is my hybrid.

Unravel the meat and lay it out flat on a board. Spread the spinach leaves out over the meat as evenly as possible. Place all the filling ingredients together in a bowl and mix well to combine. Press this mixture onto the spinach in an even layer.

Roll the meat up tightly to re-form its original shape. Push any stray filling back into the roast as you go, then tie the meat at 2cm (¾in) intervals with kitchen string.

Place all the sauce ingredients in the slow cooker dish and add the meat. Cover with the lid and cook on low for 5–6 hours or until tender.

Remove the meat from the slow cooker, place on a board and leave to rest under a tent of foil for 10 minutes. Leave the sauce cooking on the slow cooker base during this time, uncovered.

Carve the beef into thick slices and serve with the sauce spooned over and with sautéed potatoes.

I ALSO LIKE...

to use any leftover sauce to make a great soup. Blend until smooth and add vegetable stock to reach your preferred consistency.

SPECIAL OCCASIONS

MUSSELS WITH CREAM AND SAFFRON

Preparation time: 15 minutes
Cooking time: 2½–3 hours
Serves 2 as a main course or 4 as a starter

1kg (2lb 4oz) live mussels

25g (1oz) butter

1 celery stick, trimmed and finely diced

2 trimmed leeks, white part only, cleaned and finely diced

1 bay leaf

1 fresh thyme sprig

2 tsp curry powder

A pinch of cayenne pepper

A large pinch of saffron strands

250ml (9fl oz) white wine

300ml (10fl oz) fish stock

200ml (7fl oz) double cream

Sea salt and freshly ground black pepper

This recipe is fabulous for entertaining. All the preparation is done in advance, leaving you to just tip the mussels into the slow cooker shortly before your guests arrive. By the time you have had some pre-dinner drinks supper is ready.

Wash the mussels under cold running water and remove the beards or hairy bits from each one. Discard any broken or open shells and any mussels that do not close when tapped sharply on the edge of the sink.

Place the butter, vegetables, herbs and spices, wine and stock in the slow cooker dish. Cover with the lid and cook on low for 2 hours or until the vegetables are very soft.

Increase the heat to high. Leave for 15–30 minutes to warm up, then add the cream and prepared mussels. Season with salt and pepper and mix well to coat all the shells in the cooking liquid. Cover again and cook for a further 15–30 minutes or until the mussels have opened.

Stir the mussels again so that the open shells fill with the creamy sauce (discard any unopened mussels). Spoon into warm bowls and serve with crusty bread to mop up the juices.

CLASSIC BOUILLABAISSE

Preparation time: 15 minutes
Cooking time: 4½–5½ hours, plus preheating
Serves 6

700g (1lb 9oz) raw tiger prawns

1 tbsp olive oil

1 garlic clove, peeled and crushed

1 trimmed leek, cleaned and roughly chopped

1 fennel bulb, trimmed and roughly chopped

1 dried red chilli

1 bay leaf, broken

A large pinch of saffron strands

Pared rind of ½ orange

1 x 400g (14oz) tin chopped tomatoes

250ml (9fl oz) dry white wine

1.3 litres (2¼ pints) boiling water

Sea salt and freshly ground black pepper

750g (1lb 10oz) firm white fish fillets, cut into large chunks

500g (1lb 2oz) live mussels, cleaned and beards removed (see page 178)

6 tbsp roughly chopped fresh flat-leaf parsley

This glorious blend of flavours is simple to make despite the relatively long list of ingredients. Ask your fishmonger for any decent offcuts and use these in place of prime fillets, if you prefer. Rouille is available fresh or in jars from most supermarkets, good fishmongers or delicatessens.

Preheat the slow cooker on high for 30 minutes. Remove the shells from the prawns and set aside. De-vein the prawns if necessary, then put them in a large bowl, cover and leave in the fridge until needed.

Add the olive oil to the hot slow cooker dish followed by the reserved prawn shells, the garlic, leek, fennel, chilli, bay leaf, saffron and orange rind and mix well to combine. Cover with the lid and cook for 1 hour or until the shells are pink and the mixture is wonderfully fragrant.

Uncover and add all but about 2 tablespoons of the tomatoes, the wine and the boiling water. Cover with the lid and cook for a further 2–3 hours or until the vegetables have started to break down.

Ladle the mixture in batches into a food processor (including the prawn shells) and blitz until smooth. Strain through a sieve, pushing as much of the solids through as possible with the back of a ladle. Season to taste with salt and pepper and set aside in a cool place until needed.

Return the now clean slow cooker dish to the base and preheat again on high for 30 minutes. Add the strained stock, then cover with the lid and cook for a further 30–60 minutes or until piping hot.

Carefully add the fish, mussels and reserved tomatoes and prawns. Cover and cook for another 30 minutes or until the mussels have just opened and the prawns are pink. Remove and discard any mussels that have not opened. Sprinkle with the parsley and serve immediately with plenty of crusty bread to mop up the juices, and spoonfuls of rouille (see below).

I ALSO LIKE...
making my own 'cheat's' rouille. Blitz a char-grilled, peeled and deseeded red pepper in a food processor with a deseeded, chopped red chilli, ½ crushed garlic clove, 1 tablespoon of lemon juice and a few tablespoons of good-quality mayonnaise until thick. Season to taste and transfer to a serving bowl. If not using immediately, cover with cling film and store in the fridge. It should be eaten on the day it is made.

SEA BASS WITH TAMARIND AND GINGER

Sea bass is a good foil for this feisty spice paste. Packed with flavour, the paste is vibrant and zingy. The slow cooking process enables the fish to cook and marinate simultaneously, ensuring a great taste.

Using a sharp knife, slash each side of the fish about three times. Oil the inside of the slow cooker dish with some of the sesame oil.

Warm the remaining oil in a small frying pan over a low heat. When hot, add the chilli, lemongrass, ginger, garlic and lime leaves and stir-fry for 1–2 minutes or until very fragrant.

Spoon the hot mixture into a mini food processor, add the tamarind paste and coriander and blitz to make a rough paste. Spread the paste evenly over the fish. Arrange the fish in a single layer in the slow cooker dish. Drizzle over any remaining spice paste and add the cold water.

Cover with the lid and cook on low for about 3 hours or until soft when tested with the tip of a knife. Drizzle with fish sauce to taste, then divide the fish among 4 serving plates and spoon over some of the spicy cooking liquid. Serve with lime wedges and freshly cooked rice or noodles.

Preparation time: 15 minutes
Cooking time: 3 hours 5 minutes
Serves 4

2 x 900g (2lb) whole sea bass scaled, gutted and cleaned

2 tbsp sesame oil

1 red chilli, deseeded and roughly chopped

1 lemongrass stalk, peeled and roughly chopped

1 tbsp roughly chopped fresh root ginger

2 garlic cloves, peeled and crushed

4 kaffir lime leaves, roughly chopped

2 tsp tamarind paste

A small handful (about 10g/¼oz) of fresh coriander

100ml (3½fl oz) cold water

Fish sauce, to taste

Lime wedges, to serve

HERB-INFUSED BREAM WITH CARAMELISED ONIONS

Preparation time: 10 minutes
Cooking time: 3–3½ hours
Serves 4

4 x 400–500g (14oz–1lb 2oz) red bream, cleaned, scaled and gutted

4 fresh thyme sprigs

4 fresh flat leaf parsley sprigs

Sea salt and freshly ground black pepper

600g (1lb 5oz) small red onions, peeled and thinly sliced

50g (2oz) tin anchovies in olive oil

2 garlic cloves, peeled and crushed

Finely grated zest and juice of 1 lemon (preferably unwaxed)

2 tsp caster sugar

Red bream are firm-textured, well-flavoured fish that can take stronger flavourings like onions, garlic and anchovies. Choose small fish so you can serve one per person.

Score the bream three times on each side and remove the side fins with scissors. Pack the thyme and parsley into the cavities and season all over with salt and pepper.

Place the onions in the slow cooker dish. Drain the anchovies, reserving the oil, and chop as finely as possible. Mix with the garlic, anchovy oil and lemon zest and juice, then season with pepper and add the sugar. Mix into the onion mixture.

Cover with the lid and cook on high for 2 hours, stirring occasionally, until the onions are beginning to caramelise.

Arrange the fish in a single layer on top of the onions, then cover and cook for a further 1–1½ hours or until the fish is cooked through and opaque. Serve each fish on a bed of onions, with new potatoes and green vegetables.

MINI CHESTNUT, MUSHROOM AND RED WINE PIES WITH MUSTARD PASTRY

Preparation time: 35 minutes
Cooking time: 4½ hours
Serves 6
Vegetarian

---

1 tbsp olive oil

25g (1oz) butter, plus extra for greasing

350g (12oz) mushrooms, sliced

Sea salt and freshly ground black pepper

½ small onion, peeled and finely sliced

2 garlic cloves, peeled and crushed

1 tsp dried oregano

1 tbsp tomato purée

2 tbsp plain flour

200ml (7fl oz) red wine

150g (5oz) peeled cooked chestnuts

FOR THE PASTRY:

400g (14oz) self-raising flour, plus extra for dusting

A large pinch of salt

200g (7oz) vegetable suet

4 tsp wholegrain mustard

About 200–300ml (7–10fl oz) cold water

These tasty little pies are hearty and full of flavour – the fact that they're vegetarian is by the by!

Warm half of the olive oil and the butter in a large frying pan over a high heat. When hot, add the mushrooms, then season with salt and pepper and cook for 5 minutes or until golden. Spoon into a large mixing bowl. Return the pan to the heat, add the onion and garlic and cook for a further 5 minutes until golden and softened, reducing the heat if they begin to catch on the base of the pan.

Stir in the oregano, tomato purée and flour to make a thick paste. Pour in the wine and mix well. When the wine starts to boil continue stirring for another minute, then pour it into the bowl with the mushrooms. Crumble the chestnuts into the mixture, season with salt and pepper and stir to coat all the ingredients in the sauce. Set aside to cool completely.

Butter 6 mini-pudding basins that will fit in a single layer in your slow cooker dish. Line the bases with small squares of parchment paper. Butter 6 x 15 x 15cm (6 x 6in) squares of foil and set aside.

For the pastry, sift the flour and salt into a large mixing bowl. Add the suet and mix well with your hands. Mix in the mustard and enough cold water to make a soft dough.

Take about one-quarter of the dough and turn out onto a lightly floured surface. Roll out the dough until it is about 5mm (¼in) thick. Use one of the basins to cut out 6 rounds and set them aside for the pie lids.

Roll the remaining dough out until it is 5mm (¼in) thick and cut into 6 large rounds, about 13–15cm (5–6in) across. Use these to line the prepared basins, pushing down into the base of each one. Leave about 1cm (½in) pastry hanging over the top of the basins.

Spoon the cooled mushroom mixture into the lined basins. Place the reserved lids on top and fold the overhanging dough around the edges. Press together to seal, then cover with the greased foil, making a pleat in the centre as you go. Tie around the top of the basins tightly with string to stop any water getting in.

Place into the slow cooker dish and carefully pour enough boiling water around the outside to come about one-third of the way up the sides of the basins. Cover with the lid and cook on high for about 4 hours or until risen and the filling is piping hot. Remove from the slow cooker dish and leave to stand for 5 minutes. Run a sharp knife around the edges to loosen and then invert the pies onto serving plates to serve.

COQ AU VIN BLANC

Preparation time: 15 minutes
Cooking time: 8–9 hours
Serves 6

12 chicken thighs

50g (2oz) rashers streaky bacon, diced

50g (2oz) plain flour

1 large onion, peeled, halved and finely sliced

2 garlic cloves, peeled and finely sliced

500g (1lb 2oz) button mushrooms

500ml (18fl oz) dry white wine

Sea salt and freshly ground black pepper

Try this lighter version of the French classic using white wine instead of the more usual red.

Warm a large frying pan over a high heat. When hot, add the chicken thighs and bacon and cook for 5–10 minutes until golden on all sides. Spoon into the slow cooker dish. Sprinkle the flour over the meat and mix well to coat.

Return the frying pan to the heat, add the onion and garlic, reduce the heat to medium and cook for 5 minutes until the onion is softened but not coloured. Add to the chicken in the slow cooker dish.

Return the frying pan to a high heat once again and add the mushrooms – you may need to do this in a couple of batches if the pan isn't large enough. Fry for about 5 minutes for each batch or until the mushrooms are just beginning to colour. Add the wine and allow to bubble fiercely for 1–2 minutes before pouring over the chicken. Season well with salt and pepper. Cover with the lid and cook on low for 8–9 hours or until the chicken is tender and the sauce has thickened. Remove from the heat and serve with crusty bread and a green salad.

COOKING CONVENTIONALLY?
Cook in a casserole dish with a tight-fitting lid in an oven preheated to 150°C (300°F), Gas mark 2 for 4–6 hours.

MOROCCAN CHICKEN WITH PRESERVED LEMONS AND COUSCOUS

Do try to get preserved lemons for this, as it makes all the difference. If you can't, simmer a halved fresh lemon for about 8 minutes and use this. Raw lemon will be far too powerful in this dish.

Season the chicken legs with salt and pepper. Warm the olive oil and butter in a large frying pan and, when hot, add the chicken. Cook for about 5 minutes or until golden on both sides. Arrange the chicken in the slow cooker dish in a single layer and pour any cooking juices over the top.

Scatter the onions in a layer over the chicken, then add the garlic and spices. Tuck the preserved lemons between the chicken pieces and pour in enough cold water (about 150ml/5fl oz) to come halfway up the sides of the chicken. Cover with the lid and cook on low for 6–8 hours or until the chicken is tender and the sauce is wonderfully aromatic.

About 15 minutes before eating, remove the chicken from the slow cooker dish and keep warm. Add the olives and couscous to the dish and mix well. Season and cover with the lid again. Leave to steam for 10 minutes or until the couscous is tender but still has a bite (al dente).

Spoon the couscous onto warm serving plates. Top with the chicken, sprinkle with coriander and serve with a green salad.

Preparation time: 20 minutes
Cooking time: 6–8 hours
Serves 4

4 chicken legs

Sea salt and freshly ground black pepper

1 tbsp olive oil

25g (1oz) butter

2 large onions, peeled and finely diced

2 garlic cloves, peeled and crushed

1 tsp ground cinnamon

1 tsp ground ginger

4 small preserved lemons, quartered

A handful of black olives, whole or sliced

250g (9oz) couscous

Fresh coriander leaves, to garnish

BAKED GAMMON WITH ROASTED ROOT VEGETABLES AND CIDER

Preparation time: 15 minutes

Cooking time: 6-9 hours

Serves **4-6**

150g (5oz) baby carrots, scrubbed

2 parsnips, peeled and cored

1 fennel bulb, trimmed

1 red onion, peeled

300ml (10fl oz) cider

Sea salt and freshly ground black pepper

1kg (2lb 4oz) gammon joint

1 tbsp wholegrain mustard

1 tbsp clear honey

2 tbsp roughly chopped fresh flat-leaf parsley

Gammon cooks wonderfully in the slow cooker, leaving it moist and succulent. Here, a joint is cooked on a bed of root vegetables and cider for a perfect one-pot meal.

Place the baby carrots in the slow cooker dish. Cut the parsnips into 1cm (½in) wide wedges, then cut them again to make the pieces about 4cm (1½in) long. Cut the fennel and onion into thin wedges about the same thickness. Add them to the slow cooker dish together with the cider. Season generously with salt and pepper.

Place the gammon on top of the vegetables. Rub the mustard over the fat and drizzle with the honey. Cover with the lid and cook on low for 6-9 hours or until the meat is tender.

Remove the meat from the slow cooker dish and set aside on a board. Mix the parsley into the vegetables, then, using a slotted spoon, place them onto warm plates. Top with a thick slice of gammon and drizzle over the cooking juices.

I ALSO LIKE...

to use a pork shoulder or leg joint.

TURKEY WITH APPLE AND PECAN BUTTER

A turkey isn't just for Christmas – this recipe is perfect for summer celebrations and family gatherings.

Place the turkey on a large board and push your hand between the skin and the breast either side of the breastbone, to make 2 pockets. Cut 2 horizontal slices from the apple and set aside. Coarsely grate the remaining apple, place in a bowl with the lemon juice and mix well until the apple is coated in the juice. Place the butter in a large mixing bowl and mash with a fork to soften. Add the pecans, tarragon and grated apple and mix well.

Using your hand, push the flavoured butter into the 2 pockets in the turkey. Divide it evenly between either side, being sure to push the butter all the way along each breast. Finish by sliding the reserved apple slices on top of the butter, one either side of the breastbone.

Place the crown in the slow cooker dish and cook on low for 4–6 hours or until the juices run clear when the thickest part of the meat is pierced with a skewer. Lift the crown out of the dish, cover with a tent of foil and leave in a warm place to rest for at least 30 minutes, or for up to 60 minutes.

Meanwhile, carefully pour or spoon off the fat in the slow cooker dish, leaving the meaty juices behind. Pour these juices into a saucepan and bring to the boil over a high heat. Add the wine and continue to boil for another 5 minutes or until reduced by at least half. Season to taste. Serve the turkey drizzled with the buttery sauce, new potatoes and vegetables.

Preparation time: 20 minutes
Cooking time: 4–6 hours, plus resting
Serves 8–10

2–3kg (4lb 7oz–6lb 8oz) free-range turkey crown

1 red eating apple, cored

1 tbsp lemon juice

200g (7oz) unsalted butter, softened

50g (2oz) pecan nuts, finely chopped

2 tbsp chopped fresh tarragon

100ml (3½fl oz) dry white wine

Sea salt and freshly ground black pepper

CRANBERRY AND CHESTNUT FESTIVE TURKEY CROWN

Preparation time: 15 minutes
Cooking time: 4¼–6¼ hours, plus resting
Serves 8–10

2–3kg (4lb 7oz–6lb 8oz) free-range turkey crown (depending on the size of your slow cooker dish)

50g (2oz) dried cranberries

50g (2oz) cooked and peeled chestnuts

25g (1oz) smoked streaky bacon, finely diced

2 tbsp chopped fresh flat-leaf parsley

Sea salt and freshly ground black pepper

1 onion, peeled and finely sliced

100ml (3½fl oz) dry white wine

2 tbsp crème fraîche

Cooking the turkey on Christmas day seems to be a major cause of culinary stress! With a slow cooker, concerns of having a dry roast or overcooking can be allayed, as the meat stays gorgeously moist. As the breast meat takes less time to cook than the legs it makes sense to remove one or other and cook them separately for the best results.

Place the turkey on a board and push your hand between the skin and the breast, either side of the backbone, to make 2 pockets.

Place the cranberries, chestnuts and bacon into a food processor and pulse very briefly to combine the ingredients. Stir in the parsley and season to taste with salt and pepper.

Using your hands, push the cranberry stuffing into the 2 pockets that you made earlier under the turkey skin. Divide it evenly between each side, being sure to push it all the way along each breast.

Spread the onion over the base of the slow cooker dish and top with the turkey. Cover with the lid and cook on low for 4–6 hours or until the juices run clear when the deepest part of the flesh is tested with a skewer.

Lift the crown out of the dish, cover and keep in a warm place to rest for at least 15 minutes or for up to 30 minutes.

Meanwhile, skim off any excess fat from the surface of the cooking juices. Pour the remaining juices into a saucepan and bring to the boil over a high heat. Add the wine and continue to boil for another 5 minutes or until reduced by at least half. Season to taste with salt and pepper, then stir in the crème fraîche.

To serve, carefully remove the skin from the turkey breast to reveal the stuffing underneath. Spoon the stuffing onto serving plates before carving the meat. Drizzle with the creamy sauce and serve with all the usual Christmas trimmings.

I ALSO LIKE...
to use a small quantity of my chestnut and chorizo stuffing (see page 192) to push under the turkey skin instead.

EASY CHESTNUT AND CHORIZO STUFFING

Preparation time: 15 minutes
Cooking time: 4½–6½ hours, plus cooling
Serves 12

100g (3½oz) butter

1 large onion, peeled and finely diced

100g (3½oz) chorizo, finely diced

A large handful of fresh flat-leaf parsley, finely diced

250g (9oz) cooked and peeled chestnuts

300g (10oz) fresh breadcrumbs

1 x 400g (14oz) tin unsweetened chestnut purée

¼ tsp freshly grated nutmeg

2 eggs, beaten

Sea salt and freshly ground black pepper

This stuffing will cook quickly in the oven, but if you need to free up oven space on Christmas Day, as I always do, then the slow cooker is the answer. I use vacuum-packed cooked and peeled chestnuts for this recipe.

Butter the inside of the slow cooker dish generously with a quarter of the butter.

Warm a large, deep saucepan over a high heat. When hot, add the remaining butter and the onion and fry for 5 minutes or until softened. Add the chorizo and cook for a further 5 minutes or until the orangey oils start to be released. Stir in the parsley, then remove from the heat and leave to cool for 10–15 minutes or until the mixture is cool enough to handle (and won't cook the eggs you're about to add).

Crumble the chestnuts into the pan, then add the breadcrumbs, chestnut purée, nutmeg and beaten eggs. Season generously with salt and pepper, then using your hands mix everything together. Press the mixture into the slow cooker dish. Cover with the lid and cook on low for 4–6 hours or until firm.

Spoon straight from the slow cooker dish to serve.

I ALSO LIKE...
to use diced, smoked streaky bacon instead of chorizo for a variation.

POUSSIN WITH FIG AND GINGER STUFFING

These tender little birds work wonderfully with this lovely sweet fig stuffing.

Remove the string from the birds, rinse them under cold water and pat dry with kitchen paper. Season inside and out with salt and pepper. Cut half of the butter into 2 pieces. Place a piece of butter, 2 pieces of fig, ½ teaspoon of grated ginger and a sprig of thyme inside each cavity. Place the poussins in the slow cooker dish, smear the breasts with some more butter and lay 2 rashers of bacon over the top of each bird.

Melt the remaining butter in a sauté pan, add the shallots and fry over a medium-high heat for 5–10 minutes or until they become golden brown. Add the ginger wine and the remaining grated ginger and bring to the boil, then pour around the birds in the slow cooker dish. Cover with the lid and cook on low for 3–4 hours or until the juices run clear when a skewer is inserted into a leg. Remove the birds from the slow cooker and place them on an ovenproof serving plate.

Preheat the grill to its highest setting and grill the tops of the birds for 3–5 minutes or until the bacon is crispy. Keep the birds warm.

Warm a non-stick frying pan over a high heat. When hot, add the remaining fig halves cut side down and cook for 1–2 minutes or until just caramelised. Pour off some of the excess fat in the slow cooker dish, leaving just the meaty juices behind and pour these juices into the frying pan. Cook for a further 3–5 minutes or until it is reduced and slightly thickened. Season to taste, then pour the sauce around the birds.

Preparation time: 15 minutes
Cooking time: 3¼–4¼ hours
Serves 2

2 poussins, about 450–500g (1lb–1lb 2oz) each

Sea salt and freshly ground black pepper

25g (1oz) unsalted butter

3 just ripe figs, halved

2cm (¾in) piece fresh root ginger, peeled and grated

2 fresh thyme sprigs

4 rashers smoked streaky bacon

8 small shallots, peeled

400ml (14fl oz) ginger wine

BONFIRE NIGHT SAUSAGE HOTPOT

Preparation time: 15 minutes
Cooking time: 6¼–8¼ hours
Serves 8

1 tbsp olive oil

1 large onion, peeled and chopped

16 good-quality pork and herb sausages

2 red peppers, deseeded and cut into cubes

1 x 400g (14oz) tin chopped tomatoes

2 x 400g (14oz) tins mixed beans in water, rinsed and drained

2 red chillies, deseeded and finely chopped (leave the seeds in if you like it spicy!)

3 tbsp tomato purée

1 vegetable stock cube

1 tsp Worcestershire sauce

1 tsp dark muscovado sugar, plus extra to taste

2 fresh thyme sprigs

2 fresh rosemary sprigs

This easy recipe is a real crowd pleaser, especially on a cold bonfire night.

Warm the olive oil in a large frying pan over a medium heat. When hot, add the onion and fry for 5 minutes or until softened. Transfer the onion to the slow cooker dish.

Return the pan to the heat and add the sausages. Cook for 5–10 minutes until browned all over. Place them in the slow cooker together with all the remaining ingredients and mix well. Cover with the lid and cook on low for 6–8 hours or until the sauce is thick and flavoursome.

Serve with mash or baked potatoes.

I ALSO LIKE...
making this recipe with bone-in pork chops – brown them instead of the sausages, then add to the slow cooker. Cook on low for 4–6 hours.

CELEBRATION EASTER LAMB

Preparation time: 15 minutes
Cooking time: 6¼ hours
Serves 8–10

2kg (4lb 7oz) leg of lamb on the bone (or to fit in your slow cooker dish)

2 tbsp olive oil

500g (1lb 2oz) baby new potatoes, scrubbed

750g (1lb 10oz) baby carrots, scrubbed

2 red onions, peeled and cut into wedges

3 fresh mint sprigs

2 fresh rosemary sprigs

4 tbsp red wine vinegar

6 garlic cloves, peeled and roughly chopped

250ml (9fl oz) lamb stock

Sea salt and freshly ground black pepper

This all-in-one dish is ideal for a celebration or party as all the preparation is done in advance and kept contained in one pot.

Rinse the lamb under cold running water and pat dry with kitchen paper.

Warm the olive oil in a large frying pan over a high heat. When hot, add the lamb and cook for 10 minutes or until browned all over. Place the lamb in the slow cooker dish. Scatter the new potatoes around the meat, then top with the carrots and onions to surround the meat. Sprinkle over the herbs, vinegar and garlic, then pour over the stock. Cover with the lid and cook on low for 6 hours or until the meat is tender.

Remove the meat from the slow cooker, place on a board and leave to rest under a tent of foil for 5–15 minutes.

Season the vegetables to taste with salt and pepper and remove and discard the herbs. Carve the lamb and serve with the vegetables and the cooking juices spooned over.

I ALSO LIKE...

to roast a rolled shoulder of lamb in this way if I need to leave the meat for longer. The shoulder has more fat so won't dry out like the leg will over 8–9 hours of cooking.

LAMB KLEFTICO

Kleftico is a Greek dish with as many variations as you can imagine. Either way, to all intents and purposes it's a slow-cooked lamb dish with lemons, so here's another tasty version to add to the list.

Warm the olive oil in a frying pan over a high heat. When hot, add the lamb and cook until browned on all sides.

Place the onions in the slow cooker dish and top with the seared lamb. Rub the top of the lamb with the oregano and garlic and season well with salt and pepper. Pour the white wine around the outside, then surround the meat with the new potatoes and add a layer of lemon slices on top of the potatoes.

Cover with the lid and cook on low for 6–8 hours or until the potatoes are tender and the meat is piping hot. Lift the meat out of the slow cooker dish and leave to rest under a tent of foil for about 10–15 minutes before carving (although the meat will be so tender you may find a spoon and a fork more useful for serving).

COOKING CONVENTIONALLY?
Cook in a large foil parcel in an oven preheated to 170°C (325°F), Gas mark 3 for 3–4 hours or until tender.

Preparation time: **10 minutes**
Cooking time: **6–8 hours**
Serves **6**

1 tbsp olive oil

2.5kg (5lb 8oz) leg of lamb (bone in)

2 large onions, peeled and thinly sliced

1 tbsp dried oregano

2 garlic cloves, peeled and crushed

Sea salt and freshly ground black pepper

100ml (3½fl oz) white wine

600g (1lb 5oz) new potatoes

1 lemon, sliced

24-HOUR PERSIAN LAMB

Preparation time: 15 minutes
Cooking time: 24 hours
Serves 6

1.5kg (3lb 5oz) lamb shoulder, bone in (depending on the size of your slow cooker – the meat should cover the base completely)

2 large pinches of saffron strands

1 large onion, peeled and roughly chopped

2 garlic cloves, peeled and roughly chopped

3cm (1¼in) piece fresh ginger root, peeled and roughly chopped

2 large pinches of dried chilli flakes

½ tsp turmeric

1 tsp garam masala

½ tbsp cumin seeds

6 tbsp Greek yogurt

1 tbsp chopped fresh mint leaves

Cooking lamb on the bone for such a long time makes it irresistibly tender and flavoursome. This recipe has to be tried!

Place the lamb in the slow cooker dish fat side up – the meat should cover the whole of the base of the slow cooker dish.

Soak the saffron in 2 tablespoons of warm water. Meanwhile, place all the remaining ingredients (except the yogurt and mint) in a food processor and blitz to make a rough paste. Add the saffron and its soaking water and blitz again to combine. Rub the paste over the upper surface of the lamb. Cover with the lid and cook on low for 24 hours. Carefully scrape the onion mixture from the surface of the lamb before lifting the meat out onto a board or serving platter.

Mix the yogurt into the onion mixture in the slow cooker dish, being sure to scrape up any caramelised bits on the base, then mix in the mint. Use a fork and spoon to 'carve' the meltingly tender lamb and serve topped with a spoonful of the sauce and accompanied by steamed green beans.

I ALSO LIKE..

to make this with a shoulder of pork. Make sure it has the bone in and that it will fit into your slow cooker.

BEEF IN BEAUJOLAIS

Preparation time: 10 minutes
Cooking time: 8¼ hours
Serves 6–8

1.5kg (3lb 5oz) brisket joint (rolled and tied)

2 celery sticks, trimmed and diced into 5mm (¼ in) cubes

2 carrots, peeled and diced into 5mm (¼ in) cubes

1 red onion, peeled and diced into 5mm (¼ in) cubes

4 garlic cloves, peeled and crushed

1 tbsp tomato purée

1 tbsp Dijon mustard

Sea salt and freshly ground black pepper

1 bottle Beaujolais or other light red wine

250ml (9fl oz) cold water

2 tbsp redcurrant jelly, or to taste

25g (1oz) butter, chilled and diced

Brisket needs long, moist cooking to bring out its rich, sweet flavour.

Rinse the joint under cold running water and dry well with kitchen paper. Place the celery, carrot, and onion in the slow cooker dish.

Mix the garlic, tomato purée and mustard into the vegetables and season with salt and pepper. Pour in the wine and cold water and place the brisket on top of the vegetables. Cover with the lid and cook on low for 8–10 hours, basting with the red wine a couple of times. Remove the meat from the dish, cover in a tent of foil and leave to rest for 10 minutes. Meanwhile, strain the wine mixture through a sieve into a saucepan. Place the vegetables that are left behind in a bowl and keep warm.

Add the redcurrant jelly to the sauce in the pan. Bring to the boil over a high heat, then reduce the heat slightly and simmer vigorously for 10–15 minutes or until the sauce is reduced by at least half. Gradually whisk in the butter, piece by piece, until the sauce is glossy and slightly thickened.

Spoon the reserved vegetables into the centre of warm serving plates. Cut the beef into 6–8 thick slices and place a slice on top of the vegetables. Spoon the hot sauce over and serve immediately with buttered green vegetables and creamy mash.

SALT BEEF

This is a super slow recipe... you will need to start it about 11 days before you wish to eat it, but it is worth the wait!

Place the beef and half of the salt in a large freezer bag or sealed container and leave in the fridge for 12 hours. Rinse the meat under cold running water and pat dry with kitchen paper.

Place the remaining salt in a food processor with the sugar, peppercorns, coriander, juniper, bay leaves, mace and ginger and blitz to make a powder. Rub this mixture into the beef until thoroughly coated.

Place the beef in a clean freezer bag or sealed container and leave in the fridge for 5–10 days (the longer the better), turning the meat once or twice a day. Rinse the salt off the meat with cold running water.

Bring a large saucepan of water to the boil. Gently slide the meat into the water and simmer for 5 minutes. Place the carrots and celery in the slow cooker dish. Using a slotted spoon and some tongs, remove the meat from the water and place in the slow cooker on the bed of vegetables. Cover with the lid and cook on low for 6 hours or until very tender.

Remove the beef from the slow cooker and eat warm or leave to cool. Cut into thin slices to serve.

Preparation time: **20 minutes, plus 6–11 days marinating**
Cooking time: **6 hours 10 minutes**
Serves **4**

2–3kg (4lb 7oz–6lb 8oz) beef brisket, unrolled

300g (10oz) rock salt

150g (5oz) soft muscovado sugar

1 tbsp black peppercorns

1 tbsp coriander seeds

1 tbsp juniper berries

2 bay leaves

¼ tsp ground mace

½ tsp ground ginger

2 carrots, peeled and cut into chunks

2 celery sticks, trimmed and cut into chunks

TRADITIONAL OSSO BUCCO WITH GREMOLATA

Preparation time: 15 minutes
Cooking time: 12¼ hours
Serves 4

4 osso bucco (veal shin), about 1kg (2lb 4oz)

2 tbsp plain flour, for dusting

Sea salt and freshly ground black pepper

2 tbsp olive oil

25g (1oz) butter

1 small onion, peeled and very finely chopped

1 celery stick, trimmed and finely chopped

150ml (5fl oz) dry white wine

200ml (7fl oz) hot chicken or vegetable stock

FOR THE GREMOLATA:

Finely grated zest of 1 lemon (preferably unwaxed)

½ garlic clove, peeled and finely chopped

1 tbsp finely chopped fresh flat-leaf parsley

In Italian, osso bucco means 'bone with a hole'. Traditionally veal shin is used for this dish, cut horizontally through the bone, revealing the marrowbone-filled hole in the centre.

Rinse the meat under cold running water and pat dry with kitchen paper. Place the flour and some salt and pepper on a large plate. Add the meat and dust each piece to coat evenly, being careful not to dislodge any of the precious marrow.

Warm the olive oil in a large frying pan over a high heat. When hot, add the meat and cook for about 5 minutes on each side or until browned. Remove from the pan with tongs and set aside.

Reduce the heat to medium and add the butter. Add the onion, celery and a pinch of salt to the pan and cook gently, stirring frequently, for 5 minutes or until the vegetables are softened but not coloured. Tip the vegetables and any pan juices into the slow cooker dish and spread out to cover the base. Top with the meat (in a single layer if you can) and any juices that have gathered while it has been resting, then pour over the wine and stock. Cover with the lid and cook on low for 12 hours or until the meat is tender and falling off the bone.

Just before you are ready to eat, mix all the gremolata ingredients together and sprinkle it over the osso bucco before serving with creamy, Parmesan-rich polenta.

COOKING CONVENTIONALLY?
Preheat the oven to 150°C (300°F), Gas mark 2. After browning, place the meat in an ovenproof casserole dish with a tight-fitting lid and cook in the oven for 3 hours until the meat is coming off the bone, turning the meat every 20 minutes or so. When turning, lift the meat gently with a spatula so that it stays in one piece and the marrow is not lost.

STEAK, ALE AND MUSHROOM PUDDING

Preparation time: 15 minutes
Cooking time: 12–15 hours
Serves 4–6

2 tbsp olive oil

1kg (2lb 4oz) diced braising steak

250g (9oz) chestnut mushrooms, wiped and sliced

1 onion, peeled and diced

1 carrot, peeled and diced

1 celery stick, trimmed and diced

3 fresh thyme sprigs

1 tbsp tomato purée

2 tbsp plain flour

300ml (10fl oz) ale or bitter

2 bay leaves, torn in half

A knob of butter, for greasing

FOR THE PASTRY:

400g (14oz) self-raising flour, plus extra for dusting

A large pinch of salt

200g (7oz) shredded suet

2 tbsp finely chopped fresh flat-leaf parsley

About 200–300ml (7–10fl oz) cold water

This traditional steamed pudding is full of mouth-watering slow-cooked beef in a rich ale sauce.

Warm the olive oil in a large pan over a high heat. When hot, add the beef in 3–4 batches and fry until well browned. Place into the slow cooker dish and return the pan to the heat. Add the mushrooms and stir-fry for 3–5 minutes. Add the diced vegetables, thyme, purée and flour and mix. Stir in the beer and bay leaves.

Pour the mixture into the slow cooker dish, scraping up any caramelised bits from the base of the pan as you go. Cover with the lid and cook on low overnight or for about 8–10 hours until the meat is very tender and the mixture has thickened slightly. Spoon into a bowl and leave to cool completely. Discard the bay leaves.

Butter a 1.7–2 litre (3–3½ pint) pudding basin that will fit in your slow cooker dish and line the base with a small square of parchment paper. Take 2 large squares of foil about 50 x 50cm (20 x 20in) and sit one on top of the other. Butter the top sheet and set aside.

Sift the flour and salt into a large mixing bowl, add the suet and mix well with your hands, rubbing the suet in lightly. Gradually mix in the parsley and enough cold water to make a soft dough. Remove about one-quarter of the dough and set aside for the lid of the pie. Turn the remainder out onto a lightly floured surface and roll out into a 40cm (16in) round about 5mm–1cm (¼–½in) thick. Line the prepared basin with the dough, pushing it down into the base of the dish. Leave about 1cm (½in) of pastry hanging over the top of the basin.

Spoon the cooled beef mixture into the lined basin. Roll out the remaining dough into a round large enough to make a lid for the basin and place it on top of the beef mixture. Fold the overhanging dough around the edges over the top and press together to seal. Cover with the greased foil, making a pleat in the centre as you go. Tie around the top of the basin tightly with string to stop any water getting in.

Place the basin in the slow cooker dish and carefully pour enough boiling water around the outside to come about one-third of the way up the sides of the basin. Cover with the lid and cook on high for about 4–5 hours or until risen and the filling is piping hot. Remove from the slow cooker dish and leave to stand for 5 minutes. Run a sharp knife around the edge to loosen it and then invert onto a plate to serve.

BEEF IN BEER WITH HORSERADISH DUMPLINGS

Comfort food at its best – but sophisticated with it! Use fresh horseradish if you can get it, but if not, most supermarkets sell jars of good-quality grated hot horseradish.

Place the beef in the slow cooker dish and add the celery, carrots, onion, tomato purée and flour and mix well.

Pour the beer into the slow cooker dish, then add the bay leaves and season well with salt and pepper. Cover with the lid and cook on high for 6 hours or until rich and tender.

At this point start making the dumplings. Using your hands, mix the suet, flour and horseradish together in a large bowl. Season and add just enough cold water to bring the mixture together to a soft dough.

With very well-floured hands, divide the mixture into 6–8 portions and roll into balls, adding more flour to your hands as you need it. Place the dumplings around the edge of the slow cooker dish in a single layer.

Cover again and cook for a further 2 hours or until the dumplings are risen and soft. Serve immediately with plenty of seasonal green vegetables.

Preparation time: 10 minutes
Cooking time: 8 hours
Serves 6–8

1.4kg (3lb) beef leg slices (bone removed)

2 celery sticks, trimmed and diced

2 carrots, peeled and diced

1 large onion, peeled and diced

1 tbsp tomato purée

1 tbsp plain flour

500ml (18fl oz) can ale or lager

3 bay leaves, torn in half

Sea salt and freshly ground black pepper

FOR THE DUMPLINGS:

150g (5oz) shredded suet

150g (5oz) self-raising flour, plus extra for dusting

4 tsp grated horseradish

About 100ml (3½fl oz) cold water

SLOW-COOKED VENISON WITH JUNIPER, ORANGE AND WHISKY SAUCE

Preparation time: **10 minutes**

Cooking time: **8¼–9¼ hours**

Serves **4**

---

1 tbsp olive oil

400g (14oz) diced venison steak

8 shallots, peeled

250g (9oz) button mushrooms, wiped

25g (1oz) butter

1 heaped tsp juniper berries, lightly crushed

100ml (3½fl oz) whisky

2 tbsp plain flour

300ml (10fl oz) beef stock

1 fresh rosemary sprig

Juice of 1 orange

Sea salt and freshly ground black pepper

This rich dish is everything a venison casserole should be – warming, hearty and refined.

Warm the oil in a large frying pan over a medium heat, add the venison and cook for 5 minutes or until browned. Spoon the meat into the slow cooker dish.

Return the frying pan to the heat, add the shallots and mushrooms and cook for 5–10 minutes or until browned. Add the butter, juniper berries and whisky and allow to bubble for 1 minute.

Mix in the flour and half of the stock until smooth. Spoon into the slow cooker dish and add the remaining stock, the rosemary and orange juice.

Cover with the lid and cook on low for 8–9 hours or until the meat is wonderfully tender. Season to taste with salt and pepper and serve with dollops of creamy mash and steamed seasonal vegetables.

RABBIT WITH APPLE AND PRUNE SAUCE

Preparation time: **5 minutes**

Cooking time: **4 hours 10 minutes**

Serves **4**

---

3 tbsp plain flour

Sea salt and freshly ground black pepper

4 rabbit legs

1 tbsp olive oil

25g (1oz) butter

1 onion, peeled and finely sliced

2 Bramley apples peeled, cored and diced

200ml (7fl oz) brandy

150g (5oz) dried ready-to-eat prunes

This full-flavoured dish tastes like it has been prepared in a restaurant – only you will know how easy it is to make!

Place the flour in a large freezer bag and season with salt and pepper. Add the rabbit legs and toss to coat evenly. Shake the legs to remove any excess flour, but keep any leftover flour in the bag.

Warm the olive oil and butter in a large frying pan over a medium heat. When hot, add the rabbit legs and cook for 5–10 minutes or until golden brown all over. Place the rabbit legs in the slow cooker dish.

Return the frying pan to the heat, add the onion and apples plus any extra flour and mix well. Add the brandy and cook for about 1 minute. Pour over the rabbit and scatter the prunes over the top.

Cover with the lid and cook on high for 4 hours or until tender. Serve with steamed green vegetables and new potatoes.

PHEASANT WITH CIDER-BRANDY CREAM

Preparation time: 5 minutes

Cooking time: 6½ hours

Serves 4

350g (12oz) pheasant thigh fillets (about 8)

25g (1oz) plain flour

Sea salt and freshly ground black pepper

1 tbsp olive oil

1 onion, peeled, halved and finely sliced

1 Bramley apple, peeled, cored and diced

100ml (3½fl oz) cider brandy, such as Calvados or dry cider

100ml (3½fl oz) boiling water

2 bay leaves, halved

2 tbsp double cream

Pheasant is relatively low in fat and can dry out quickly so a slow cooker's moist heat is perfect for retaining its succulence.

Place the pheasant in a large freezer bag with the flour. Season generously with salt and pepper before sealing the bag and tossing everything together until the meat is completely coated. Warm the olive oil in a large frying pan over a high heat. Add the pheasant and cook for 2 minutes on each side until just golden. Remove from the pan and place in the slow cooker dish.

Return the frying pan to the heat, add the onion and cook for 5 minutes, stirring frequently and reducing the heat if necessary, until golden brown. Mix in any remaining flour from the freezer bag and add the apple. Cook for a further minute or until thickened.

Stir the cider brandy into the onion mixture, scraping up any bits from the base of the pan as you do so. Allow to bubble for 30–60 seconds or until the brandy has reduced almost completely. Mix in the boiling water to loosen the mixture, then spoon the contents of the pan into the slow cooker dish. Add the bay leaves.

Cover with the lid and cook on low for 6 hours or until the pheasant is tender and the sauce is thick. Pour in the cream and fold into the sauce, adding a splash of boiling water if the sauce is too thick. Season to taste and serve with mounds of creamy mash.

SAUCES, CHUTNEYS + JAMS

TOMATO KETCHUP

Preparation time: 25 minutes
Cooking time: 6½–8½ hours, plus cooling
Makes 1kg (2lb 4oz)
Vegetarian

1.5kg (3lb 5oz) ripe tomatoes, roughly chopped

2 onions, peeled and sliced

½ large red pepper, deseeded and chopped

Sea salt and freshly ground black pepper

50g (2oz) soft brown sugar

100ml (3½fl oz) cider vinegar

1 tsp English mustard

1 cinnamon stick

1 tsp whole allspice

1 tsp whole cloves

1 tsp blade mace

1 tsp celery seeds

1 tsp black peppercorns

1 bay leaf

½ garlic clove

Paprika, to taste (optional)

3–4 heaped tsp cornflour

1–2 tbsp cold water

Long, slow cooking suits tomatoes, drawing out all their flavour and sweetness; so for home-made ketchup slow cookers are perfect.

Combine the tomatoes, onion and chopped pepper in the slow cooker dish. Season well with salt and pepper, then cover with the lid and cook for 3–4 hours, stirring occasionally, until very soft. Remove and clean the cooker dish. Strain through a sieve using the back of a ladle to push as much through as possible. Return the mixture to the slow cooker dish. Add the sugar, vinegar and mustard.

Tie the cinnamon, allspice, cloves, mace, celery seeds, peppercorns, bay leaf and garlic in a square of muslin. Drop it into the mixture and cook, uncovered, on high for 3–4 hours, stirring occasionally until thickened.

Season to taste, adding paprika if you like. Mix the cornflour with enough cold water to form a paste, then add it to the mixture and stir well. Cook, uncovered, for a further 30 minutes or until thick and the mixture no longer tastes floury. Allow to cool. Remove the bag of spices, then pour the mixture through a funnel into sterilised bottles. Seal and store in the fridge for up to a month.

ONION AND ALE BURGER RELISH

Preparation time: 10 minutes
Cooking time: 5-7 hours, plus cooling
Makes about 1kg (2lb 4oz)
Vegetarian

1 tbsp olive oil

3 onions, peeled, halved and sliced

1 garlic clove, peeled and finely sliced

75g (3oz) dark soft brown sugar

Sea salt and freshly ground black pepper

2 red chillies, deseeded and finely chopped

1½ tbsp wholegrain mustard

250ml (9fl oz) ale

6 tbsp white wine vinegar

Perfect for burgers or equally good with bangers and mash.

Place the olive oil, onions, garlic and 25g (1oz) of the sugar in the slow cooker dish. Season with salt and pepper, then cover with the lid and cook on high, stirring occasionally, for 2–3 hours or until the onions are caramelised and golden.

Add the remaining ingredients, then cook, uncovered, for 3–4 hours or until thick and almost all of the liquid has evaporated.

Allow to cool, then spoon into sterilised jars, seal and store in the fridge for up to three months.

COOKING CONVENTIONALLY?
Place in a non-reactive saucepan, cover with a lid and cook on the hob for 1 hour in step 1 and then for a further 30 minutes in step 2.

TOMATO CHUTNEY

Preparation time: 10 minutes
Cooking time: 5 hours, plus cooling
Makes about 500g (1lb 2oz)
Vegetarian

1kg (2lb 4oz) tomatoes, peeled, deseeded and chopped

3 tbsp soft light brown sugar

1 tbsp mustard seeds

2 tbsp red wine vinegar

3 tbsp olive oil

Sea salt and freshly ground white pepper

If you grow your own, this is a great recipe for using up the glut of summer tomatoes.

Place the tomatoes, sugar, mustard seeds, vinegar and olive oil in the slow cooker dish and mix well. Season generously with salt and white pepper.

Cover with the lid and cook on high, stirring occasionally, for 2 hours until the tomatoes are very soft.

Remove the lid and continue cooking for a further 3 hours, stirring occasionally, until thick and jammy.

Pour the chutney into sterilised jars and allow to cool. Seal and store in the fridge for up to a month.

I ALSO LIKE...
adding some dried chilli flakes for a chutney with more of a kick.

MANGO CHUTNEY

This chutney is an essential accompaniment to curry and poppadums, but it is also great with strong cheeses and cold meats.

Place the mangoes in the slow cooker dish and add the vinegar, sugar, salt and raisins.

Place the ginger, chilli, garlic, cumin, coriander and turmeric into a mini blender and blitz to combine into a rough paste.

Add the paste to the mango mixture and mix in together with the cinnamon stick, star anise, kalonji seeds and vegetable oil.

Cover with the lid and cook on low for 3–4 hours or until thickened. Allow to cool, then remove the cinnamon and star anise. Spoon into sterilised jars, cover with wax disks and store in the fridge for up to a month.

TRY...
You can buy kalonji (black onion) seeds from good supermarkets or Asian food stores. They are worth purchasing, as they give the chutney a unique and authentic flavour.

Preparation time: 15 minutes
Cooking time: 3–4 hours, plus cooling
Makes 1kg (2lb 4oz)
Vegetarian

3 firm mangoes, peeled, stoned and cut into 2cm (¾in) pieces

125ml (4fl oz) white wine vinegar

75g (3oz) caster sugar, plus extra to taste

1½ tsp salt, or to taste

50g (2oz) raisins

2cm (¾in) piece fresh root ginger, peeled

1 bird's eye chilli

3 garlic cloves, peeled

1 tsp ground cumin

1 tsp ground coriander seeds

½ tsp turmeric

1 cinnamon stick

2 star anise

1 tbsp kalonji (black onion) seeds

2 tbsp vegetable oil

LIME PICKLE

Preparation time: 5 minutes
Cooking time: 8–10 hours, plus cooling
Serves 8
Vegetarian

---

4 limes, cut into quarters or eighths

---

1 tbsp salt

---

1 tbsp groundnut oil

3cm (1¼in) piece fresh root ginger, peeled and sliced

---

1 tbsp white vinegar

1–2 green chillies, finely diced

About 3 tbsp caster sugar

---

1 tbsp paprika

---

1 tsp garam masala

---

1 tsp cumin seeds

---

2 garlic cloves, peeled and finely sliced

An essential accompaniment to curries, lime pickle takes quite a long time to make, needing several days or weeks to marinate in salt. Ironically, in this instance, a slow cooker actually speeds up the process! This is great with poppadums or to accompany a curry.

Place the limes in the slow cooker dish with all the remaining ingredients and mix thoroughly.

Cover with the lid and cook on low for 8–10 hours, stirring occasionally, until thickened. If it remains fairly liquid, then remove the lid and cook for a further hour. Add more sugar to taste, although be careful as the mixture will be very hot.

Carefully spoon into sterilised jars and allow to cool, then seal and store in the fridge for a week before eating. It must be eaten within a month.

TRY...
adjusting the seasoning with sugar after cooking to get the best results.

CHRISTMAS CHUTNEY

Preparation time: 15 minutes
Cooking time: 5–6 hours
Makes 4 x 500ml (18fl oz) jars
Vegetarian

750g (1lb 10oz) Bramley cooking apples, peeled, cored and sliced

Juice of 1 lemon

1 onion, peeled and diced

500g (1lb 2oz) fresh cranberries

200g (7oz) dried ready-to-eat figs, trimmed and diced

Finely grated zest and juice of 1 orange

200g (7oz) caster sugar

200g (7oz) soft light brown sugar

1 tsp ground allspice

½ tsp ground ginger

500ml (18fl oz) red wine vinegar

2 tsp sea salt

When I first graduated, I worked in a very posh London food hall. One of my first assignments was to develop some new products, the first of which was a Christmas chutney. It is still being sold to this day! Of course, I wouldn't dream of revealing the top-secret recipe in these pages, but here's a not-so-secret version!

Place the apples in the slow cooker dish with the lemon juice and mix until the apples are coated. Add all the remaining ingredients and mix well. Poke any apple into the mixture so that it isn't in contact with the air (this will prevent the mixture from going too brown).

Cover with the lid and cook on high for 4 hours, then remove the lid and cook for a further 1–2 hours or until thick and the fruit has broken down.

Mix the chutney well with a wooden spoon, then divide between 4 sterilised 500ml (18fl oz) jars (see page 218). Seal and store in a cool, dark place for a minimum of two months or for up to a year (the longer the better to enable the flavours to mature).

I ALSO LIKE...

to vary the dried fruit in this recipe – prunes, dates and raisins all work well.

HOT CHILLI SAUCE

This fiery sauce is fantastic! If you prefer a milder version then reduce the number of chillies and remove the seeds too. This sauce is great with burgers, sausages and anything that needs a bit of a kick!

Place all the ingredients except the cornflour, vinegar and vegetable oil into the slow cooker dish and stir well.

Cover with the lid and cook on low for about 8 hours until the vegetables are very soft. Remove the lid and increase the temperature to high for the last hour of cooking.

Stir the cornflour into the vinegar to make a paste, then add it to the slow cooker dish together with the oil. Leave uncovered, stirring occasionally, for 20–30 minutes or until thickened.

Allow to cool, then pour the mixture into a food processor in batches and blitz until smooth. Pour into sterilised bottles, seal and store in the fridge for up to a month.

Preparation time: 10 minutes
Cooking time: 9–10 hours, plus cooling
Makes about 900ml (1½ pints)

10 plum tomatoes, peeled
1 tbsp caster sugar
5 garlic cloves, peeled and roughly chopped
1 tbsp Worcestershire sauce
2 tsp salt
2–3 jalapeño peppers or other hot chillies, roughly chopped
2 onions, peeled and roughly chopped
1 tsp chilli powder
1 tsp dried oregano
1 tsp dried thyme
1 tsp cornflour
1 tbsp white wine vinegar
1 tbsp vegetable oil

GREEN CHILLI JAM

A tasty, zingy savoury jam, which is great with cheeses, meats, salads and sausages and particularly good with pork pies.

Using a sharp knife, cut the chillies in half lengthways, then deseed and chop the flesh finely.

Place the chillies in the slow cooker dish together with the onion, garlic, ginger, vegetable oil and sugar. Cover with the lid and cook on low for 2 hours, stirring occasionally, until the vegetables have softened and are just starting to caramelise.

Add the vinegar and stir well. Leave uncovered and continue to cook for about 1 hour or until the liquid evaporates slightly.

Mix in the fish sauce to taste. Spoon into sterilised jars, allow to cool, then seal and store in the fridge for up to a month.

I ALSO LIKE...
using red chillies when I want it a bit hotter.

Preparation time: 15 minutes
Cooking time: 3 hours, plus cooling
Makes 250g (9oz)

12 large green chillies
1 onion, peeled and very finely diced
2 garlic cloves, peeled and finely chopped
6cm (2½in) piece fresh root ginger, peeled and finely chopped
100ml (3½fl oz) vegetable oil
2 tsp caster sugar
100ml (3½fl oz) white wine vinegar
1 tbsp Thai fish sauce, to taste

FIG CHUTNEY

Preparation time: 10 minutes
Cooking time: 4–5 hours, plus cooling
Makes 1kg (2lb 4oz)
Vegetarian

1kg (2lb 4oz) fresh figs

350g (12oz) soft dark brown sugar

250ml (9fl oz) cider vinegar

2 tbsp chopped fresh root ginger

Sea salt and freshly ground black pepper

1 small onion, peeled and diced

1 tsp black mustard seeds

¼ tsp ground cinnamon

A pinch of ground cloves

This is a simple spiced chutney, which is perfect to accompany cheeses, cured meats and crusty bread.

Using a sharp knife, trim the stems from the figs and cut the fruit into quarters. Place the sugar, vinegar, ginger, 2 teaspoons of salt, the onion and spices in the slow cooker dish and mix well. Cover with the lid and cook on low for 3 hours.

Season to taste with salt and pepper, adding more spices if necessary. Remove the lid and increase the temperature to high. Cook for a further 1–2 hours or until thickened.

Spoon the mixture into sterilised preserving jars (see tip) and allow to cool. Cover with wax disks and keep in the fridge for up to three months.

TRY...

All jams, preserves, chutneys and relishes must be potted in very clean containers. Wash jars and bottles thoroughly in hot soapy water and dry in a warm oven preheated to 150°C (300°F), Gas mark 2 (make sure you don't put any plastic seals or lids in the oven as they will melt). After drying, handle the jars and bottles as little as possible and leave on a clean tea towel. When the jam or chutney is cooked, pour the hot mixture into the prepared containers while they are still warm – this will lessen the chance of the glass cracking – and fill them almost to the top.

RED ONION MARMALADE

Preparation time: 15 minutes
Cooking time: 6–8 hours, plus cooling
Makes 1kg (2lb 4oz)
Vegetarian

2kg (4lb 8oz) red onions, peeled, halved and thinly sliced

4 garlic cloves, peeled and thinly sliced

150g (5oz) butter

4 tbsp olive oil

150g (5oz) caster sugar

1 tbsp fresh thyme leaves

A pinch of dried chilli flakes (optional)

Sea salt and freshly ground black pepper

75cl bottle red wine

350ml (12fl oz) sherry vinegar or red wine vinegar

200ml (7fl oz) port

Soft, sticky onion marmalade – great with pâtés (such as the Farmhouse Pâté on page 29) salads or cooked meats like steak and duck.

Place the onions and garlic in the slow cooker dish together with the butter and olive oil and mix well to combine. Sprinkle with the sugar, thyme leaves, chilli flakes (if using) and some salt and pepper. Cover with the lid and cook on high, stirring occasionally, for 3–4 hours or until very soft and caramelised.

Add the wine, vinegar and port and cook, uncovered, for a further 3–4 hours, stirring occasionally, until thick and a dark brown colour.

Allow to cool, then spoon into sterilised jars and seal. Eat straight away or store in the fridge for up to three months.

I ALSO LIKE…
making this jam with ordinary brown onions, especially if you have some that need using up.

SWEET AND SOUR PICKLED ONIONS

If you're a fan of pickled onions you'll love this easy recipe. These onions are great served with cold meats and salads and are rather good in Cheddar cheese sandwiches too.

Place the onions in a large bowl and cover with boiling water. Leave to stand for 5 minutes, then drain and peel off the skins. Place the peeled onions in the slow cooker dish.

Add the remaining ingredients to the slow cooker dish, then cover with the lid and cook on high for 3 hours or until the onions are soft.

Spoon the mixture into sterilised jars. Allow to cool, then seal and store in the fridge for up to three months.

COOKING CONVENTIONALLY?
Place all the ingredients in a large saucepan, cover with a lid and cook over a very low heat for 2–3 hours, checking that the liquid has not evaporated and adding more cold water as required.

Preparation time: 15 minutes
Cooking time: 3 hours
Makes 1kg (2lb 4oz)
Vegetarian

30 small white onions

2 tbsp tomato purée

100ml (3½fl oz) red wine vinegar

2 tbsp olive oil

2 tbsp caster sugar

1 bay leaf

250ml (9fl oz) dry white wine

250ml (9fl oz) water

100g (3½oz) raisins

200ml (7fl oz) cold water

PICKLED PLUMS

This is almost a sauce really and can be served warm or cold. Either way it tastes great, as the slow cooking really concentrates the plums' flavour. Try it with meats, burgers or your favourite sausages.

Mix all of the ingredients together in a bowl, cover and chill for at least 12 hours or preferably overnight.

When the plums have marinated, pour the contents of the bowl into the slow cooker dish. Cover with the lid and cook on low for 10–12 hours or until starting to caramelise slightly.

Use the plums warm or pour into sterilised jars and allow to cool, then seal and store in the fridge for up to three weeks.

COOKING CONVENTIONALLY?
At step 2 pour the contents of the bowl into a roasting tray and cook in an oven preheated to 140°C (275°F), Gas mark 1 for 6–8 hours until caramelised. Remove from the oven and set aside until needed or continue from step 3.

Preparation time: 10 minutes, plus marinating
Cooking time: 10–12 hours, plus cooling
Makes about 1kg (2lb 4oz)
Vegetarian

12 just ripe plums

100g (3½oz) caster sugar

Finely grated zest and juice of 1 orange

Juice of 1 lemon

1 tsp pickling spice

½ cinnamon stick

1 green chilli, deseeded and finely diced

1 tbsp red wine vinegar

CLASSIC MARMALADE WITH WHISKY

Preparation time: 15–20 minutes
Cooking time: 2¼ hours, plus cooling
Makes **about 700g (1lb 9oz)**
Vegetarian

450g (1lb) oranges (about 4), preferably Seville, halved

300ml (10fl oz) cold water

450g (1lb) granulated or jam sugar

2 tbsp whisky

The slow cooker is perfect for softening up the orange rind when making marmalade.

Place a saucer in the freezer to chill. Squeeze the juice from the oranges and place in the slow cooker dish. Reserve the pips, pith and peel.

Using a sharp knife, shred the peel finely into strips about 1cm x 3mm (½ x ⅛in) in size. If the pith is very thick, trim some off to a maximum of 5mm (¼in).

Add the peel to the slow cooker dish together with the cold water. Tie the pips and pith in a square of muslin and add as well. Cover with the lid and cook on high for 2 hours or until the peel is very soft.

Tip the mixture into a heavy-based saucepan, add the sugar and heat gently, stirring constantly, until dissolved. Bring to a rapid boil and cook for 15 minutes. Dab a spoonful of marmalade onto the frozen saucer and leave for 30 seconds before pushing your finger through it. If the surface of the mixture wrinkles it is ready. If not, return to the heat and boil for slightly longer, then re-test.

Remove the pan from the heat and lift out the muslin bag with a spoon. Leave to stand for 15 minutes, then stir in the whisky.

Spoon the marmalade into hot sterilised jars and cover with wax discs. Allow to cool, then seal and store in a cool, dry place for up to six months. Once opened, keep in the fridge and use within three weeks.

COOKING CONVENTIONALLY?
Use a large saucepan and place over a low heat.

LIME AND LEMONGRASS CURD

Curds are wonderfully easy to make, but they do need lots of constant attention when being made conventionally. The slow cooker removes the need to watch over the mixture, making it fabulously easy.

Place the lime zest and juice in a medium-sized saucepan. Using a rolling pin, bash the lemongrass lightly to bruise it, then add it to the pan together with the butter.

Warm the pan over a low-medium heat until the butter has melted, then add the sugar. Remove from the heat and stir until the sugar has dissolved completely. Allow to cool slightly, then remove the lemongrass and discard.

Whisk the eggs in a large heatproof bowl that fits into your slow cooker dish. Gradually whisk in the lime mixture, whisking constantly, then cover the bowl tightly with foil.

Place the bowl in the slow cooker dish and carefully pour enough boiling water around the outside to come about halfway up the sides of the bowl. Cover with the lid and cook on low for 3–4 hours or until thick and glossy.

Beat the mixture well with a wooden spoon until completely smooth, then ladle into sterilised jars and cover with wax discs. Leave to cool, then seal and store in the fridge for up to three weeks.

I ALSO LIKE...
using other citrus fruit, such as oranges or lemons, or a combination of both.

Preparation time: **5 minutes**
Cooking time: **3–4 hours, plus cooling**
Makes **about 1kg (2lb 4oz)**
Vegetarian

Finely grated zest and juice of 4 limes

1 lemongrass stalk, outer layers removed

100g (3½oz) butter

450g (1lb) caster sugar

4 medium eggs

APPLE AND MINT JELLY

Preparation time: 10 minutes, plus straining
Cooking time: 2¼–3 hours, plus cooling
Makes about 2kg (4lb 8oz)
Vegetarian

1.5kg (3lb 5oz) Bramley cooking apples, unpeeled, cored and roughly chopped

25g (1oz) fresh mint, leaves only

1 cinnamon stick

750ml (1¼ pints) cold water

100g (3½oz) chopped baby spinach

300ml (10fl oz) cider vinegar

500g–1kg (1lb 2oz–2lb 4oz) preserving sugar

Making your own jelly is very satisfying. Buy jelly bags and muslin from cook shops (online sites have a wide selection).

Place a saucer in the freezer ready for testing the jelly. Place the apples in the slow cooker dish with all but about one-quarter of the mint leaves and the cinnamon stick. Add the cold water, cover with the lid and cook on high for about 1 hour, stirring occasionally until soft and thick. Add the spinach, stir to combine, then pour in the cider vinegar. Cook, uncovered, for a further hour. Spoon the mixture into a jelly bag (follow the instructions on the pack) and leave to strain over a bowl overnight – don't be tempted to press this through the muslin; leave until the dripping stops.

Wrap the remaining mint leaves in a small muslin bag. Measure the amount of drained apple and spinach juice and place in a large saucepan. Add 500g (1lb 2oz) of preserving sugar for every 600ml (1 pint) of juice. Discard the pulp in the jelly bag.

Place the pan over a medium heat and stir until the sugar has dissolved. Add the bag of mint, then bring to a rapid boil and leave, boiling away, for 10 minutes or until reduced slightly. Remove from the heat and set aside for a couple of minutes. Dab a spoonful of jelly onto the frozen saucer and leave for 30 seconds before pushing your finger through it. If the surface of the jelly wrinkles it is ready. If not, return to the heat and boil for slightly longer, then re-test. Remove any scum from the surface with a large spoon, then pour into sterilised jars, cover with wax discs and allow to cool.

APRICOT AND CARDAMOM JAM

Preparation time: 10 minutes
Cooking time: 4½–5½ hours, plus cooling
Makes about 1kg (2lb 4oz)
Vegetarian

500g (1lb 2oz) dried ready-to-eat apricots

20 cardamom pods

200g (7oz) golden granulated sugar

750ml (1¼ pints) cold water

This is a bit of a cheat's jam really, but still gives a great result. Cardamom and apricots are a great combination, as the spice just gives the fruit a little edge of fragrance and warmth. This is great with scones or spread in the middle of a Victoria sandwich.

Place the apricots in a food processor and blitz until finely chopped – if your blender struggles with this add a spoonful or two of water to loosen the mixture.

Using a small sharp knife, cut the cardamom pods open to reveal the small black seeds. Remove the seeds and discard the husks. Add the seeds to the food processor and blitz again to combine.

Spoon the mixture into the slow cooker dish and add the sugar and cold water. Stir well for about 1 minute or until the sugar starts to dissolve, then cover with the lid and cook on high for 2½ hours, stirring twice during cooking, until slightly thickened.

Remove the lid and continue cooking for 2–3 hours, stirring occasionally, until thick. The contents of the slow cooker will be extremely hot so caution should be taken throughout this time.

Ladle into sterilised jars and cover with wax discs. Leave until completely cold then seal and store in the fridge for up to three weeks.

I ALSO LIKE...
using other dried fruit, such as figs, prunes or pears.

LOW-SUGAR FIG AND GINGER JAM

Jam is usually made with equal quantities of fruit and sugar, but slow cooking enables you to use less sugar, although your jam will be a little runnier than normal.

Place a saucer in the freezer to chill. Place the figs and lemon in the slow cooker dish with the sugar, cold water and ginger.

Cover with the lid and cook on low for 2½ hours or until starting to thicken, stirring twice during cooking.

Remove the lid and increase the temperature to high. Cook for a further 2–3 hours or until the jam is thick.

Remove the saucer from the freezer. Take a teaspoon of the jam and place it onto the saucer. Allow to cool slightly for 1–2 minutes, then push a finger lightly through the jam. If the surface wrinkles it is ready. If not, return to the heat and boil for slightly longer, then re-test.

Ladle the jam into sterilised jars, cover with wax discs and allow to cool, then seal and store in the fridge for up to two months.

TRY...

If you can't get fresh figs use the Apricot and Cardamom Jam recipe on page 226, using dried figs in place of the apricots and add some ginger to the mixture instead of cardamom pods.

Preparation time: **10 minutes**
Cooking time: **5–6 hours, plus cooling**
Makes **1kg (2lb 4oz)**
Vegetarian

1kg (2lb 4oz) fresh figs, stemmed and cut into quarters

1 lemon, very finely sliced

500g (1lb 2oz) jam sugar with pectin

125ml (4fl oz) cold water

2 tbsp chopped stem ginger

LOW-SUGAR STRAWBERRY AND VANILLA JAM

Preparation time: 10 minutes
Cooking time: 5½–7 hours, plus cooling
Makes 1kg (2lb 4oz)
Vegetarian

1kg (2lb 4oz) strawberries

500g (1lb 2oz) jam sugar with pectin

2 tbsp lemon juice

A pinch of sea salt

1 vanilla pod

Normally, jam requires equal quantities of fruit to sugar to set properly, but the slow cooking of this recipe allows the mixture to use less sugar. Your jam won't be as firm as some but you will have used 50 per cent less sugar.

Place a saucer into the freezer to chill. Wash and drain the strawberries, then hull. Cut any large fruit into smaller pieces.

Place the strawberries in the slow cooker dish with the sugar, lemon juice and salt. Crush lightly with a potato masher or fork and leave to stand for 15 minutes or until the sugar has dissolved.

Using a small sharp knife, split the vanilla pod in half lengthways and scrape out the seeds. Add these and the pod to the slow cooker dish. Cover with the lid and cook on high for 2½ hours, stirring twice during cooking, until beginning to thicken.

Remove the lid and continue to cook for a further 3–4 hours, stirring occasionally, until thick.

Remove the saucer from the freezer and place a teaspoonful of the jam onto it. Leave for a minute or two and then push an index finger through it. If the surface of the jam wrinkles it is ready. If not, cook for another 30 minutes and re-test. Using a pair of tongs, remove the vanilla pod. Be careful as it will be very hot.

Ladle the jam into sterilised jars, cover with wax discs and allow to cool completely. Seal and store in the fridge and use within two months.

AMAZING HOT CHOCOLATE SAUCE

This super-easy sauce is a chocoholic's dream! It's rich and delicious – perfect for spooning, drizzling or dipping, and if you leave it to go cold it will solidify into a dense, truffle-like mousse.

Place all the ingredients in a heatproof bowl that will fit into your slow cooker dish. Pour enough cold water into the slow cooker dish around the bowl to come about one-third of the way up the sides of the bowl. Cover with the lid and cook on low for 1 hour.

Beat well to combine and then leave on the warming function for up to an hour before use. Spoon over sundaes or profiteroles, or dip in fruit and biscuits as a sweet fondue.

I ALSO LIKE...
to pour the mixture into little ramekins or espresso cups and leave to cool. The sauce will set into an intense, gooey chocolate pot.

Preparation time: **5 minutes**
Cooking time: **1–2 hours**
Serves **6 as a chocolate pot and 8–10 as a sauce**
Vegetarian

200g (7oz) plain dark chocolate, broken into pieces

100g (3½oz) milk chocolate, broken

6 marshmallows, roughly chopped

300ml (10fl oz) half-fat crème fraîche

150ml (5fl oz) skimmed milk

2 tbsp Baileys liqueur (optional)

BRANDY SAUCE

It is easy to make brandy sauce on the hob but it requires constant stirring. This method couldn't be easier and leaves you free to do other things.

Place the brandy and cornflour in the slow cooker dish and mix well to make a paste. Slowly stir in the milk, cream and sugar. The mixture must cover the base of the slow cooker by at least 2cm (¾in) to prevent it from burning. Cover with the lid and cook on low for 2 hours or until thickened. Whisk well to combine and serve.

I ALSO LIKE...
to use this method with Grand Marnier, Cointreau or other liqueurs.

Preparation time: **2 minutes**
Cooking time: **2 hours**
Serves **6**
Vegetarian

2 tbsp brandy

1 tbsp cornflour

250ml (9fl oz) whole milk

100ml (3½fl oz) double cream

2 tbsp caster sugar, or to taste

REAL VANILLA CUSTARD

Preparation time: 5 minutes
Cooking time: 2–3 hours
Serves 6–8
Vegetarian

1 vanilla pod

1 tsp cornflour

300ml (10fl oz) double cream

3 large egg yolks

25g (1oz) caster sugar

Real custard is easy enough to make on the hob but it needs constant attention and stirring for a good 10–15 minutes before it starts to thicken. This method looks after itself in the slow cooker.

Using the tip of a small sharp knife, cut the vanilla pod in half lengthways. Scrape the seeds out of the pod and place them in a 1 litre (1¾ pint) heatproof bowl (check that the bowl fits into your slow cooker first) together with the now empty pod.

Place the cornflour in a small dish and mix in a little of the cream, until there are no lumps. Pour this into the bowl with the vanilla, add the remaining cream, egg yolks and sugar and whisk well.

Cut a piece of parchment paper into a round just larger than the top of the bowl. Dampen under cold water and scrunch it up into a loose ball (this will make it easier to handle). Place the drained disc of parchment directly on the surface of the egg mixture, pushing it down around the edges to create a seal.

Place a trivet or upturned saucer in the base of the slow cooker dish and pour in just enough cold water to cover it and position the bowl on top. Cover with the lid and cook on low for 2–3 hours or until thickened.

Carefully remove the bowl from the slow cooker and place on a heatproof surface. Whisk well and remove the vanilla pod before serving.

I ALSO LIKE...
to keep the vanilla pod (it will still have plenty of flavour), rinse it in some clean water and dry with kitchen paper, then embed it in a jar of caster sugar, cocoa or coffee to impart a gorgeous vanilla flavour.

PUDDINGS
+
CAKES

PEARS POACHED WITH AMARETTO AND VANILLA

Preparation time: **5 minutes**

Cooking time: **4-6 hours**

Serves **6**

Vegetarian

6 medium pears

Juice of 1 lemon

2 tbsp caster sugar

100ml (3½ fl oz) Amaretto liqueur

About 500ml (18fl oz) cold water

1 vanilla pod, split lengthways

The slow cooker is perfect for poaching fruit as it is a very gentle form of cooking and will stop the fruit breaking up and disintegrating.

Using a small paring knife, carefully remove the core from the base of each pear, then peel the pears leaving the stalks intact. Place them in the slow cooker dish and sprinkle with the lemon juice, carefully turning the fruit until it is well coated in the juice.

Sprinkle with the sugar and add the Amaretto, enough cold water to cover the pears and the vanilla pod, then place a piece of greaseproof paper over the fruit to keep it immersed in the liquid.

Cover with the lid and cook on low for 4-6 hours or until the pears are completely tender when tested with the tip of a small sharp knife.

Remove the fruit with a slotted spoon. Strain the poaching liquid into a small pan and warm over a high heat. Bring to the boil and leave to boil vigorously until the liquid is reduced by about half, or until thick and syrupy. Serve the fruit hot or cold with the syrup drizzled over.

I ALSO LIKE...

using halved, stoned, unpeeled apricots.

MARZIPAN-BAKED APPLES

Baked apples are so redolent of cold autumnal days. The slow cooker makes the most of the apple flavour by allowing it to develop gradually without the apples overcooking, while the marzipan stuffing flavours them from within.

Using a corer, remove the core from each of the apples, then, using a small sharp knife, lightly score a horizontal line around the middle of each apple.

Mix the remaining ingredients, except the cold water, in a bowl using the back of a wooden spoon to blend everything together. Divide the mixture evenly among the holes in the apples, pressing it down until it is all used up.

Stand the apples in the slow cooker dish and add the cold water. Cover with the lid and cook on low for 3–4 hours or until the apples are soft and the filling is hot. Serve with any cooking juices drizzled over and plenty of cream or custard.

Preparation time: 10 minutes
Cooking time: 3–4 hours
Serves 4
Vegetarian

4 medium Bramley cooking apples

25g (1oz) dates, chopped

25g (1oz) walnut pieces

50g (2oz) soft light brown sugar

50g (2oz) natural golden marzipan, softened

A large pinch of mixed spice

4 tbsp cold water

SLOW-POACHED STRAWBERRIES WITH PIMM'S AND CLOTTED CREAM

Combine three classic summer ingredients to make this stunningly simple dessert.

Place the strawberries in the slow cooker dish and add the sugar, Pimm's and cold water. Cover with the lid and cook on low for 1–2 hours or until the strawberries are very soft but still holding their shape.

Serve the strawberries topped with dollops of clotted cream and a crisp biscuit or two on the side.

I ALSO LIKE...
using other summer fruits and berries in season.

Preparation time: 5 minutes
Cooking time: 1–2 hours
Serves 4
Vegetarian

800g (1lb 12oz) strawberries, washed and hulled

100g (3½oz) caster sugar, or to taste

200ml (7fl oz) Pimm's

100ml (3½ fl oz) cold water

MIDDLE EASTERN FRUIT AND NUT SALAD

Preparation time: **5 minutes**
Cooking time: **4-6 hours**
Serves **6-8**
Vegetarian

400g (14oz) dried apricots

100g (3½oz) prunes

100g (3½oz) raisins

100g (3½oz) blanched almonds

50g (2oz) pistachios

Juice of 1 orange

2 tbsp clear honey, or to taste

Orange blossom water, to taste

Pomegranate seeds, to serve

Use dried apricots and prunes for this tasty recipe, not the ready-to-eat varieties – these have already been soaked and will disintegrate during cooking.

Place the dried fruits and nuts in the slow cooker dish. Pour in just enough cold water to come one-third of the way up the fruit. Drizzle over the orange juice and honey. Cover with the lid and cook on low for 4–6 hours or until thickened and syrupy.

Add enough orange blossom water to taste, and some more honey if required. Serve with vanilla ice cream and scatter over the pomegranate seeds.

I ALSO LIKE...
to cook fresh apricots in the same way when they're in season, but I leave out the prunes if I'm doing this.

WINTER FRUIT SALAD

Preparation time: 10 minutes
Cooking time: 2¼ hours
Serves 4-6
Vegetarian

300ml (10fl oz) grenadine

450ml (15fl oz) cold water

50g (2oz) caster sugar

1 vanilla pod, split lengthways

3 pears, quartered and cored

4 seasonal eating apples, quartered and cored

6 plums, quartered and stoned

100g (3½oz) blackberries, fresh or frozen

This warm fruit salad is great on its own or as an accompaniment to another dessert. The grenadine gives the fruit a wonderful colour and flavour. You can buy it from most supermarkets, drink specialists or from online suppliers.

Place the grenadine, cold water, sugar and vanilla pod in the slow cooker dish and add the pears, apples and plums. Cover with a layer of greaseproof paper to ensure that the fruit is completely immersed in the liquid and can't pop above the surface.

Cover with the lid and cook on low for 2 hours or until the fruit is tender when tested with the tip of a knife. Mix in the blackberries and leave to stand for 5 minutes.

Using a slotted spoon, transfer the fruit into a serving dish. Pour the cooking liquid into a pan, bring to the boil over a high heat and boil vigorously for 5–10 minutes or until reduced by half. Serve the poached fruit warm or cold with ice cream or cream and the thickened sauce spooned over.

COOKING CONVENTIONALLY?
Place all the ingredients in an ovenproof baking dish and cook in an oven preheated to 150°C (300°F), Gas mark 2 for 50 minutes or until the fruit is softened.

APRICOTS WITH VANILLA

These delicate, velvety little fruits always seem to disappoint when eaten raw. Slow cooking them coaxes out their unique flavour making them utterly irresistible. Check that your slow cooker is happy on the warming function overnight – read the manufacturer's instructions.

Place the apricots in the slow cooker dish. Peel the lemons with a vegetable peeler and add the peel to the apricots together with the juice of half a lemon. Mix gently until the fruit is completely coated in the juice, then pour in enough cold water to cover and add the sugar.

Using a small sharp knife, cut the vanilla pod in half lengthways and scrape the seeds out with a knife into the slow cooker, then add the pod.

Cover with the lid and cook on the warming function overnight or for up to 9 hours until the apricots are meltingly soft. Serve hot just as they are with a little of the syrup, or with muesli and yogurt.

I ALSO LIKE...
making a syrup. Remove the apricots after cooking and pour the syrup into a small saucepan. Bring to the boil over a high heat and simmer for 10 minutes or until reduced and thickened. Spoon the syrup over the apricots and serve.

Preparation time: **10 minutes**
Cooking time: **6–9 hours**
Serves **4**
Vegetarian

10 fresh apricots, halved and stoned

2 lemons (preferably unwaxed)

225g (8oz) caster sugar

1 vanilla pod

CARAMELISED PEACHES WITH BASIL CREAM

Preparation time: **5 minutes**

Cooking time: **2–3 hours**

Serves **6**

Vegetarian

6 just ripe peaches

50g (2oz) caster sugar

4 tbsp sweet dessert wine (keep the rest of the bottle to serve with dessert)

300ml (10fl oz) single cream

6 basil leaves

These soft caramelised peaches are fabulous with this delicate, subtly flavoured basil cream.

Using a sharp knife, cut the peaches in half and remove the stones, then dip the cut side of the fruit into the sugar to coat.

Place the fruit cut side down in the slow cooker dish and drizzle with the wine. Cover with the lid and cook on low for 2–3 hours or until soft and starting to caramelise.

Meanwhile, pour the cream into a small saucepan and warm over a low heat, stirring occasionally to make sure that it is not sticking to the base of the pan. Do not allow to boil, but when hot, remove from the heat. Add the basil leaves and set aside to cool completely.

Remove the basil from the cream and discard. Serve the peaches cut side up with the cream spooned over and a crisp biscuit on the side.

I ALSO LIKE...

using other seasonal stone fruit, too.

STICKY PLUM CAKE

Preparation time: **15 minutes**
Cooking time: **2 hours, plus
preheating and standing time**
Serves **8**
Vegetarian

**200g (7oz) softened butter, plus
extra for greasing**

**100g (3½oz) caster sugar, plus
1 tbsp extra for dusting**

6 plums, halved and stoned

100g (3½oz) self-raising flour

1 tsp baking powder

100g (3½oz) ground almonds

100g (3½oz) soft dark brown sugar

4 medium eggs, beaten

**This moist cake is great eaten cold on its own or warm as a
pudding with custard.**

Remove the slow cooker dish from the base. Turn the slow cooker
base (without the dish in it) on to high to preheat. Butter and line
the sides and base of the slow cooker dish with parchment paper,
paying particular attention to the corners. Dust the base of the
dish with the tablespoon of caster sugar.

Place the plums flat side down in the slow cooker dish.

Sift the flour and baking powder into a large bowl. Add all the
remaining ingredients and mix until smooth. Don't worry if it
curdles slightly, it won't affect the finished cake. Pour over the
plums and insert the slow cooker dish on the preheated base.
Cover with the lid and cook on high for 2 hours or until the edges
are springy to the touch (the middle will still be soft).

Remove the dish from the base and leave to stand on a heatproof
surface with the lid on for 30 minutes. Carefully invert onto a
plate and remove the parchment paper. Eat warm or cold.

I ALSO LIKE...
using halved apricots instead of plums.

ORANGE AND ALMOND LOAF CAKE

Make sure the loaf tin will fit in the slow cooker first; alternatively, if you have a smaller machine, make this cake in ramekins or individual pudding basins (adjust the cooking time accordingly).

Butter a non-stick 500g (1lb 2oz) loaf tin with butter and line the base with parchment paper. Place a trivet or upturned saucer in the base of the slow cooker and pour enough cold water around it to just cover the top, about 250ml (9fl oz).

Cream the butter and sugar together in a large bowl until light and fluffy. Slowly add the eggs, beating well between each addition. Fold in the flour, ground almonds and baking powder, then slowly stir in the milk and the orange zest.

Scatter the flaked almonds over the base of the prepared tin, then spoon the sponge into the tin and level the surface with the back of the spoon. Cover tightly with a lightly buttered piece of foil, butter side down.

Place in the slow cooker on top of the trivet or saucer and cover with the lid. Cook for 3–3½ hours or until risen and spongy to the touch.

Remove from the slow cooker and leave to stand on a heatproof surface for a minute or so. Run a sharp knife around the sponge before inverting onto a wire rack and leave to cool completely. Using a serrated knife, cut into thick slices and serve with lashings of cream or crème fraîche.

I ALSO LIKE...

to vary this recipe with fruit instead of the flaked almonds – scatter 50g (2oz) berries, such as raspberries, over the base before topping with the cake mixture.

Preparation time: 10 minutes
Cooking time: 3–3½ hours
Serves 4
Vegetarian

100g (3½oz) butter, softened, plus extra for greasing

100g (3½oz) golden caster sugar

2 medium eggs, beaten

50g (2oz) self-raising flour

50g (2oz) ground almonds

½ tsp baking powder

4 tbsp semi-skimmed milk

Finely grated zest of 1 orange

50g (2oz) toasted, flaked almonds

BLUEBERRY AND LIME LOAF CAKE

Preparation time: 10 minutes

Cooking time: 3–3½ hours

Serves 4

Vegetarian

100g (3½oz) butter, softened, plus extra for greasing

100g (3½oz) golden caster sugar

2 medium eggs, beaten

50g (2oz) self-raising flour, sifted

50g (2oz) ground almonds

½ tsp baking powder

4 tbsp semi-skimmed milk

Finely grated zest of 1 lime

100g (3½oz) blueberries

This simple cake is fabulously light and full of flavour, and it also looks great. Blueberries work brilliantly with the lime but raspberries, blackberries and loganberries also work well too.

Butter a non-stick 500g (1lb) loaf tin and line the base with parchment paper. Place an upturned saucer or trivet into the slow cooker dish and pour enough cold water around it to just cover the top (about 250ml/9fl oz).

Cream the butter and sugar together in a large mixing bowl until light and fluffy. Slowly add the eggs, beating well between each addition. Fold in the flour, almonds and baking powder, then slowly stir in the milk and the lime zest.

Place enough blueberries in the base of the tin to just cover the bottom. Fold the remainder into the sponge mixture, then spoon the sponge into the tin and level the surface with the back of the spoon.

Place the tin in the slow cooker on top of the saucer or trivet and cover with the lid. Cook on high for 3–3½ hours or until risen and spongy to the touch.

Remove the tin from the slow cooker and leave to stand for a minute or so before turning out. Run a sharp knife around the sponge before inverting and leaving to cool completely on a wire rack. Using a serrated knife, cut into thick slices and serve with lashings of cream.

COOKING CONVENTIONALLY?
Bake this cake in an oven preheated to 170°C (325°F), Gas mark 3 for 50 minutes or until spongy to the touch.

LEMON UPSIDE-DOWN PUDDING

Preparation time: 20 minutes
Cooking time: 1½ hours
Serves 6
Vegetarian

100g (3½oz) butter, softened

175g (6oz) caster sugar

3 lemons

4 eggs, separated

50g (2oz) plain flour

500ml (18fl oz) semi-skimmed milk

There are so many variations of this recipe in existence – this one is a family hand-me-down relied on frequently for Sunday lunches over the generations. Here, it adapts amazingly to slow cooking, producing a particularly light sponge floating on a pool of dreamy, zingy lemon custard – a conventional oven should never be used for this recipe again!

Butter a 2 litre (3½ pint) shallow baking dish just a little smaller than the slow cooker dish with some of the butter. Place the rest in a bowl, add the sugar and mix with an electric whisk until pale and fluffy.

Finely grate the zest from 2 of the lemons and add it to the blended butter and sugar, then add the juice of all 3 lemons. Mix everything together – don't worry, the mixture should curdle at this point.

Mix in the egg yolks and flour, followed by the milk to make a runny batter. In a clean bowl, using clean utensils, whisk the egg whites until firm, then fold them gently into the batter.

Place the prepared dish in the slow cooker dish and pour enough cold water around the outside until it comes about halfway up the sides. Pour the lemon mixture into the prepared dish. Cover with the lid and cook on high for 1½ hours or until just set but still wobbly in the centre.

Carefully remove the dish and serve immediately with dollops of crème fraîche, if you like.

I ALSO LIKE...
using limes instead of lemons, or a mixture of both.

SWEET ORANGE AND RICOTTA CHEESE CAKES

Light, fluffy, more-ish – and very easy to make.

Butter 6 x 200ml (7fl oz) ramekins. Finely grate the zest from the orange and set aside.

Place the brandy, sultanas, juice of the orange and the cardamom seeds into a saucepan and bring to the boil over a high heat. Reduce the heat and simmer for 5 minutes. Allow to cool slightly.

Whisk the ricotta, cornflour, eggs and caster sugar together with the reserved orange zest. Add the cooled sultana mixture and any remaining liquid from the pan.

Pour the mixture into the prepared ramekins, filling them to the very top and place them in the slow cooker dish. Carefully pour enough boiling water around the outside to come about one-third of the way up the sides of the dishes.

Cover with the lid and cook on high for 2–3 hours or until risen and just set. Remove and allow to cool for a couple of minutes before serving, hot or cold, dusted with icing sugar and with dollops of crème fraîche on the side.

I ALSO LIKE...
using a lemon or lime instead of the orange.

Preparation time: 10 minutes
Cooking time: 2–3 hours
Serves 6
Vegetarian

Butter, for greasing

1 orange

50ml (1¾fl oz) brandy

50g (2oz) sultanas

Seeds from 6 cardamom pods, slightly crushed

350g (12oz) ricotta cheese

2 tsp cornflour, sifted

3 large eggs

100g (3½oz) caster sugar

Icing sugar, for dusting

ST CLEMENTS CHEESECAKE

Preparation time: 15 minutes
Cooking time: 2¼ hours, plus
preheating, cooling and chilling
Serves 6-8
Vegetarian

FOR THE CHEESECAKE:

375g (13oz) ricotta cheese

300g (10oz) full-fat cream cheese

2 tsp cornflour

200g (7oz) caster sugar

75g (3oz) cut mixed peel (optional)

4 eggs, beaten

4 eggs yolks, beaten

**Finely grated zest of 2 lemons
(preferably unwaxed)**

FOR THE SYRUP:

225g (8oz) caster sugar

125ml (4fl oz) orange juice

1 lemon

This creamy cheesecake is studded with tangy citrus peel and tastes great. If you're not a fan of peel, though, just leave it out.

Cover the base of the slow cooker dish with 1cm (½in) water, then cover with the lid and turn the slow cooker base on to high to preheat.

Butter a deep 18–20cm (7–8in) round non-stick cake tin and line the base and sides with parchment paper (make sure the tin fits into your slow cooker dish first – a 20cm/8in oval dish would work too if this fits your slow cooker more comfortably, or use 6 x 150ml/5fl oz ramekins).

To make the cheesecake, beat the ricotta and cream cheese together in a large bowl until smooth. Add the cornflour and sugar and mix well to combine. Fold in the dried fruit, whole eggs, egg yolks and the finely grated lemon zest.

Carefully place the cake tin in the slow cooker dish, cover with the lid and bake on high for 2 hours or until just set in the centre. Turn off and leave to cool in the water bath. Remove the tin from the slow cooker, place on a heatproof surface and leave to cool completely. When cold, cover and chill in the fridge overnight.

To make the syrup, place the sugar and orange juice in a heavy-based saucepan over a low heat and stir to dissolve. Increase the heat and bring to the boil. Using a zester, remove the zest from the lemon in long strands and add these to the boiling syrup. Boil for 10–12 minutes or until syrupy. Remove from the heat and leave to stand for 5 minutes before serving drizzled over generous slices of the cheesecake.

RHUBARB AND CUSTARD POTS

Preparation time: 15 minutes

Cooking time: 3–4 hours, plus preheating and cooling

Serves 6

Vegetarian

A knob of butter, for greasing

200g (7oz) rhubarb, cut into 2cm (¾in) pieces

25g (1oz) caster sugar, plus extra to taste

Finely grated zest and juice of 1 orange

FOR THE CUSTARD:

2 eggs

2 egg yolks

500ml (18fl oz) double cream

75g (3oz) golden caster sugar

A winning combination made even better with slow cooking. The slow poaching of the fruit coaxes out the wonderful flavour of the rhubarb, while the moist conditions in the slow cooker create a wonderfully light custard.

Butter the slow cooker dish and add the rhubarb. Add 25g (1oz) of the sugar and the orange zest and juice. Cover with the lid and cook on low for 1–2 hours or until soft. Add more sugar to taste and set aside for several hours to cool completely.

Preheat the slow cooker by turning it on high and butter 6 x 200ml (7fl oz) ovenproof ramekins. Divide the cooled rhubarb mixture between the dishes.

Put the eggs and yolks into a 1 litre (1¾ pint) measuring jug and whisk well. Mix in the cream and sugar, then pour the custard mixture into the dishes.

Place the ramekins in the slow cooker dish and carefully pour enough boiling water around the outside to come about halfway up the sides of the dishes. Cover with the lid and cook on high for 2 hours. Remove the ramekins from the water bath and leave to stand on a heatproof surface for 5 minutes before serving.

MINI COCONUT CUPS WITH MANGO AND LIME

I use espresso cups for this recipe, but you could also use teacups or ramekins if you prefer.

Give the tin of coconut milk a good shake before opening it. Pour it into a large saucepan and warm over a medium heat. When it is just below boiling point remove it from the heat.

Meanwhile, whisk the sugar and eggs together in a large bowl. Gradually pour the warm coconut milk over the top, whisking as you pour. Place 8 espresso cups in the slow cooker dish, leaving a space to pour the water in.

Strain the coconut custard through a sieve into a jug and divide the custard between the cups. Carefully pour enough boiling water around the outside to come about one-third of the way up the sides of the cups. Cover with the lid and cook on low for 2 hours or until just set.

Carefully remove the cups from the water bath, place on a heatproof surface and leave to cool completely.

Meanwhile, place the mango in a bowl and stir in the lime zest and enough juice to taste. Set aside at room temperature until ready to serve.

Serve each coconut cup on a saucer with a spoonful of the colourful mango salad on top.

I ALSO LIKE...
to make these custards with whole milk instead of coconut milk, topping them with seasonal fresh fruit – strawberries and/or raspberries work well.

Preparation time: **5 minutes**
Cooking time: **2¼ hours**
Serves **8**
Vegetarian

1 x 400g (14oz) tin full-fat coconut milk

100g (3½oz) caster sugar

4 eggs

1 mango, peeled, stoned and cut into 5mm (¼in) cubes

Finely grated zest and juice of 1 lime

PLUM AND GINGER PUDDINGS

Preparation time: **15 minutes**

Cooking time: **2–3 hours**

Serves **8**

Vegetarian

150g (5oz) butter, softened, plus extra for greasing

175g (6oz) dark brown soft sugar

3 eggs, beaten

150g (5oz) self-raising flour

3 pieces stem ginger in syrup

4 plums, halved and stoned

These dainty little puddings are warming and comforting to eat but remarkably light. Serve with ginger syrup, but the custard, cream or ice cream should also always be close to hand!

Cut 8 squares of foil, about 15 x 15cm (6 x 6in) in size. Butter one side of the foil and 8 mini pudding basins. Line the base of each basin with a small square of parchment paper and save the foil for later.

Beat 150g (5oz) of the sugar with the butter in a large mixing bowl with an electric mixer until very pale and fluffy. Gradually add the eggs and then the flour. Strain the stem ginger, reserving about 3 tablespoons of the syrup. Dice the ginger according to taste – either finely or in larger pieces if preferred.

Sprinkle the reserved sugar onto a plate and dip the cut side of each of the plum halves into the sugar to coat thickly. Press each one, cut side down, into the base of each basin.

Divide the cake mixture among the 8 basins and level the surface of each one. Cover the basins tightly with the prepared foil squares and place in the slow cooker dish. Carefully pour enough boiling water around them to come about halfway up the sides of the basins. Cover with the lid and cook on high for 2–3 hours or until the sponge feels springy to the touch.

Remove the basins from the slow cooker and leave to rest for 2–3 minutes. Use a sharp knife to loosen the edge of each sponge, then turn out. Drizzle with the reserved ginger syrup and serve with spoonfuls of crème fraîche.

BAILEYS BREAD AND BUTTER PUDDING

Preparation time: 30 minutes

Cooking time: 2–3 hours

Serves 6

Vegetarian

12 large slices brioche

Butter, for greasing

150ml (5fl oz) whole milk

200ml (7fl oz) double cream

100ml (3½fl oz) Baileys

75g (3oz) caster sugar

2 eggs

1 egg yolk

6 tsp demerara sugar

Fruit or no fruit in bread and butter pudding? Purists will adore this fruitless pudding with layers of buttery brioche floating in a rich Baileys-flavoured custard.

Use a 200ml (7fl oz) ramekin to stamp out 24 circles of brioche and set aside. Butter 6 x 200ml (7fl oz) ramekins and divide the brioche rounds among the ramekins in layers.

Whisk the milk, cream, Baileys, caster sugar, eggs and yolk together in a bowl. Pour the custard mixture slowly over the brioche, giving it a chance to soak in between each addition.

Place the ramekins in the slow cooker dish and carefully pour enough boiling water around them to come about halfway up the sides of the dishes. Cover with the lid and cook on high for 2–3 hours or until just firm.

Remove the ramekins from the water bath and scatter with the demerara sugar before serving.

CHERRY CLAFOUTIS

A wonderful dessert prepared quickly and simply and then left to its own devices in the slow cooker. The English cherry season is so short and lacking in supply that this recipe uses a jar of cherries, but do use fresh stoned cherries if you can get them.

Drain the cherries in a sieve or colander, reserving the juice or brandy that they have been stored in.

Remove the slow cooker dish from the base and preheat the base on high. Butter the slow cooker dish, then scatter the cherries over the base of the dish.

Melt the butter in a small saucepan over a medium heat, then remove from the heat and allow to cool slightly. In a large mixing bowl, mix the eggs with the yolks and sugar.

Whisk in the cooled melted butter, followed by the flour and the milk until smooth, then pour over the cherries.

Place the slow cooker dish in the preheated base and cover with the lid. Cook for 2–3 hours or until just set in the centre. Pour the reserved juice or brandy into a small pan and bring to the boil over a high heat. Cook until it is reduced by about half, then serve drizzled over the clafoutis.

COOKING CONVENTIONALLY?
Place in a baking dish and bake in an oven preheated to 190°C (375°F), Gas mark 5 for 45–50 minutes or until golden brown and just set.

Preparation time: 15 minutes
Cooking time: 2–3 hours, plus preheating
Serves 6
Vegetarian

700g (1lb 9oz) jar of cherries in natural juice or brandy

50g (2oz) butter, plus extra for greasing

4 medium eggs

2 egg yolks

125g (4½oz) caster sugar

75g (3oz) plain flour, sifted

600ml (1 pint) whole milk

BLACKBERRY AND APPLE ROLY-POLY

Preparation time: 20–25 minutes
Cooking time: 2–3 hours
Serves 6–8

150g (5oz) fresh blackberries

1 eating apple, peeled, cored and diced

1 tbsp icing sugar

Butter, for greasing

300g (10oz) self-raising flour, plus extra for dusting

150g (5oz) shredded suet

75g (3oz) caster sugar

Finely grated zest of 1 lemon

175–200ml (6–7fl oz) whole milk

Cold water or milk, for brushing

This roly-poly should not be relegated to winter – it has a very light texture and the addition of lemon zest makes it rather zingy too.

To make the filling, warm the blackberries, apple and icing sugar together in a saucepan over a medium heat until the fruits begin to soften. Increase the heat, bring to the boil and cook for 5–10 minutes or until the juices thicken and become jammy. Pour the mixture into a bowl and leave to cool.

Butter and lightly flour a large sheet of parchment paper, about 40 x 30cm (16 x 12 in), and place it on a larger sheet of foil.

To make the dough, mix the flour, suet, caster sugar and lemon zest together in a large bowl. Stir in enough milk until the mixture forms a soft dough, then gather together into a ball, but don't overwork or knead it as it will become tough.

On a lightly floured surface, roll the dough into a rectangle about 22 x 25cm (8½ x 10in). Spread with the cooled blackberry mixture, leaving a 2cm (¾in) border around the edge, and moisten the border with a little cold water or milk. Starting from one of the shorter ends of dough, begin rolling into a tight cylinder. With the seam underneath, lay the roly-poly in the centre of the parchment paper. Fold over the long paper and foil edges to seal, leaving enough space above the pudding to allow it to rise. Squeeze the paper ends together tightly to seal them.

Scrunch a large piece of foil into a thick cushion about the same size as the roly-poly and place this in the base of the slow cooker dish. Lay the parcel on top and carefully pour enough boiling water around it to just cover the foil cushion and come to the base of the roly-poly. Cover with the lid and cook on high for 2–3 hours or until firm to the touch.

Remove from the slow cooker and leave to rest for a minute or two before unwrapping. Use a serrated knife to cut it into thick slices and serve immediately with vanilla custard.

SIX-HOUR CINNAMON RICE

Preparation time: 5 minutes
Cooking time: 6 hours
Serves **8**
Vegetarian

125g (4½oz) pudding or risotto rice

125g (4½oz) caster sugar

1 tsp ground cinnamon

1 litre (1¾ pints) whole milk

250ml (9fl oz) double cream, plus extra to serve

1 bay leaf, broken

50g (2oz) toasted almonds, chopped

I absolutely love rice pudding! Here is an indulgent version using double cream. I am a fan of cinnamon and bay, but if you're not, then you can happily omit them without spoiling the flavour.

Place a 2 litre (3½ pint) ovenproof dish in the slow cooker dish (or adjust the size and ingredients to fit your slow cooker dish).

Place the rice in the dish. Stir in the sugar, cinnamon, milk and cream, then add the bay leaf. Carefully pour enough boiling water around the outside to come about one-third of the way up the sides of the dish. Cover with the lid and cook on low for 6 hours or until the rice is tender and the cinnamon has crusted on the surface to form a brown skin.

Scatter the almonds over the dish and eat immediately with extra cream. Great with a fruit compote.

COOKING CONVENTIONALLY?
Cook in a 2 litre (3½ pint) ovenproof dish for 5 hours in an oven preheated to 140°C (275°F), Gas mark 1.

CRUNCHY VANILLA CRÈME CARAMELS

These dainty desserts are a variation on a traditional crème caramel.

Line a baking sheet with a piece of non-stick parchment paper. Set 4 x 250ml (9fl oz) ovenproof teacups to one side (or use ramekins of the same size).

Place the granulated sugar in a heavy-based saucepan together with the water and warm over a high heat. Do not stir the mixture but swirl the pan occasionally until the sugar dissolves. Bring to the boil and cook for 7–10 minutes or until golden.

Pour a quarter of the caramel onto the prepared baking sheet and leave to cool completely. When cold, cover and leave at room temperature until needed.

Meanwhile, spoon the remaining caramel into the teacups. Don't wash up the pan, as you will need it for the custard mixture.

Pour the milk, cream and vanilla into the caramel saucepan. Warm over a medium heat for 10 minutes, stirring frequently, until any caramel has dissolved, and the mixture is just below boiling point. Remove from the heat and leave to stand while you prepare the eggs.

Place the eggs, egg yolks and caster sugar in a large bowl and whisk together well. Slowly pour the hot milk mixture over the top, whisking continuously as you pour. Strain the mixture through a sieve into a large jug, then pour into the caramel-lined cups.

Place the cups in the base of the slow cooker dish and carefully pour enough boiling water around the outside to come about one-third of the way up the sides of the cups.

Cover with the lid and cook on low for 2½ hours (or on high for 1½ hours) or until the custard is just set in the centre.

Remove the cups from the water bath and leave to cool completely on a heatproof surface before chilling in the fridge overnight.

Just before eating, place the now solid caramel on the baking sheet in a freezer bag and bash with a wooden rolling pin to break into shards.

Loosen the edges of the custards with the tip of a sharp knife, then invert onto plates. Scatter the caramel shards over the tops before serving.

I ALSO LIKE...
adding a touch of brandy or Cointreau to the custard before pouring it into the cups.

Preparation time: 15 minutes
Cooking time: 1 hour 40 minutes–2 hours 40 minutes, plus cooling and chilling
Serves 4
Vegetarian

100g (3½oz) granulated sugar

150ml (5fl oz) cold water

350ml (12fl oz) milk (skimmed is fine if you want to cut down on fat)

200ml (7fl oz) double cream

1 tsp vanilla extract

2 medium eggs

3 medium egg yolks

25g (1oz) caster sugar

CARDAMOM CRÈME BRÛLÉE

Preparation time: 15 minutes, plus infusing

Cooking time: 2–3 hours, plus chilling

Serves 4

Vegetarian

568ml (1 pint) tub double cream

3 cardamom pods, crushed

6 egg yolks

7 tbsp golden caster sugar

Cardamom is a wonderfully fragrant, warming spice, and it works amazingly in this easy but sophisticated brûlée.

Warm the cream and cardamom pods over a low heat to just below boiling point. Remove from the heat and set aside for 30 minutes to infuse.

Return the pan to the heat and warm again to just below boiling point. Whisk the egg yolks and 3 tablespoons of the sugar together in a large bowl, then slowly whisk the hot cream into the egg mixture, whisking constantly to prevent the eggs from scrambling.

Strain the custard through a sieve into a large jug, then pour into 4 x 200ml (7fl oz) ramekins. Place the dishes in the slow cooker dish and carefully pour enough boiling water around them to come about halfway up the sides of the ramekins.

Cover with the lid and cook on high for 2–3 hours or until just firm. Remove the ramekins from the slow cooker and leave to cool completely, then cover and chill in the fridge for at least 2 hours, but preferably overnight.

Preheat the grill to its highest setting. Sprinkle the remaining caster sugar over the top of each custard and place under the grill for 3–5 minutes or until the sugar is golden. Remove from the grill and leave for 1 minute before serving.

RICH CHOCOLATE AND HAZELNUT PUDDING

Preparation time: 15 minutes
Cooking time: 2 hours 10 minutes, plus preheating
Serves 8
Vegetarian

250g (9oz) unsalted butter, plus extra for greasing

200g (7oz) dark plain chocolate (at least 70% cocoa solids), broken into pieces

50g (2oz) chopped roasted hazelnuts

2 tbsp Frangellico liqueur (hazelnut liqueur), optional

100g (3½oz) cocoa powder, sifted

75g (3oz) self-raising flour, sifted

1 tsp baking powder

350g (12oz) caster sugar

5 medium eggs, beaten

Our friends Sam and Toby are addicted to the hazelnut liqueur Frangellico, so this one is for them.

Remove the slow cooker dish from the base. Butter the dish well and line with a double layer of parchment paper. Turn the slow cooker base (without the dish in it) on to high to preheat.

Melt the butter and chocolate in a large heatproof bowl over a saucepan of simmering water. Mix until smooth, then remove the bowl from the heat, add the hazelnuts and Frangellico (if using) and stir well.

In a separate bowl, mix the cocoa powder, flour, baking powder and sugar together. Add this to the melted chocolate mixture and stir well. Beat in the eggs until smooth.

Pour the mixture into the prepared slow cooker dish. Cover with the lid and carefully place the dish on the preheated slow cooker base. Cook for about 2 hours on low or until the centre is just set.

Remove from the base and leave to stand uncovered for about 10 minutes before serving warm with ice cream. Alternatively, leave to cool completely before cutting into chunky pieces and serving.

FAB FOR THE FREEZER
Cut the cooked and cooled pudding into portions and freeze. Defrost from frozen in the microwave for 1 minute on high or until hot and softened throughout.

DOUBLE CHOCOLATE AND PEAR PUDDING

This intensely chocolaty pudding with pear is made with a sauce on the top and sponge underneath. As it cooks it magically swaps around, leaving a pool of gooey chocolate in the bottom of the dish.

Cover the base of the slow cooker dish with 1cm (½in) water, then cover with the lid and turn the slow cooker base on to high to preheat. Butter a 1 litre (1¾ pint) ovenproof serving dish (make sure it will fit into your slow cooker dish first, or use four 200ml (7fl oz) ovenproof ramekins).

Sift the flour and half of the cocoa powder into a large bowl. Add the caster sugar and mix together.

Whisk the cooled, melted butter, egg and milk together in a small bowl, then pour over the flour mixture and whisk together well. Fold in the pear and spoon the mixture into the prepared serving dish.

In a separate bowl, mix the remaining cocoa and the brown sugar together. Sprinkle this over the mixture in the serving dish. Carefully place the pudding in the warm water in the slow cooker. Spoon 4 tablespoons of freshly boiled water evenly over the top of the pudding and pour any remainder around the outside to come one-third of the way up the sides of the pudding. Cover with the lid and cook on high for 1½ hours or until a skewer inserted halfway into the pudding comes out clean.

Remove the pudding from the slow cooker. Dust with more cocoa powder and serve immediately with crème fraîche or ice cream. Best eaten straight away.

Preparation time: 10 minutes
Cooking time: 1½ hours, plus preheating
Serves 4
Vegetarian

50g (2oz) butter, melted and cooled, plus extra for greasing

100g (3½oz) self-raising flour

3 tbsp cocoa powder, plus extra for dusting

125g (4½oz) golden caster sugar

1 medium egg

4 tbsp milk

1 ripe pear, peeled, cored and diced

50g (2oz) soft dark brown sugar

GOOEY CHOCOLATE PUDDING

Preparation time: **15 minutes**
Cooking time: **2–3 hours, plus preheating**
Serves **6–8**
Vegetarian

75g (3oz) unsalted butter, plus extra for greasing

100g (3½oz) plain dark chocolate, broken into pieces

100g (3½oz) self-raising flour

100g (3½oz) ground almonds

50g (2oz) caster sugar

A pinch of salt

2 large eggs

2 egg yolks

175ml (6fl oz) whole milk

100g (3½oz) white chocolate, cut into chunks

This pudding is rich and dark with a soft molten centre as long as it's not overcooked, when it will revert back to being a chocolate sponge. So, for the best results, serve it while the middle is still wobbly and gooey . This pudding is great served with crème fraîche and summer berries.

Remove the slow cooker dish and preheat the slow cooker base on high. Butter the inside of the dish liberally. Place the plain dark chocolate in a heatproof bowl set over a saucepan of simmering water and leave to melt. Make sure the bowl doesn't touch the water.

Sift the flour and almonds into a large bowl, add half of the sugar, the salt, eggs, yolks and milk and whisk until smooth.

Add the remaining butter to the now melted chocolate and mix well. Leave until the butter has melted completely, then slowly pour the melted chocolate and butter into the egg mixture, whisking as you go. Fold in the white chocolate.

Pour the mixture into the slow cooker dish, place it in the preheated cooker base and cover with the lid. Cook for 2–3 hours or until set around the edges but still wobbly in the centre. Remove the slow cooker dish from the base and leave to stand for 5 minutes before serving.

EXTRA TOFFEE BANOFFEE PUDDING

Preparation time: 15 minutes
Cooking time: 2 hours, plus preheating
Serves 6–8
Vegetarian

75g (3oz) butter, melted, plus a little extra for greasing

125g (4½oz) self-raising flour

Pinch of salt

1½ tsp baking powder

100g (3½oz) golden caster sugar

2 bananas

250ml (9fl oz) milk

1 medium egg, lightly beaten

1 tsp vanilla extract

125g (4½oz) soft dark brown sugar

3 tbsp golden syrup

250ml (9fl oz) boiling water

I love banoffee pie, but this gooey, indulgent pudding takes my enjoyment to a whole new level!

Remove the slow cooker dish from the base and grease with a little butter. Turn the slow cooker base (without the dish in it) on to high to preheat.

Sift the flour, salt and baking powder into a bowl and add the sugar. In a small dish, mash one of the bananas with a fork and add it to the bowl together with the milk, melted butter, egg and vanilla and whisk well.

Cut the other banana into 2cm (¾in) pieces and arrange in a single layer in the base of the slow cooker dish. Pour the mixture over the top.

Place the brown sugar, golden syrup and boiling water in a bowl and stir until the sugar dissolves. Pour this mixture over the cake mix in the dish. Cover with the lid and carefully place the dish on the preheated slow cooker base. Cook on high for 2 hours.

Remove from the heat and leave to stand uncovered for 5–10 minutes before spooning into bowls. Serve with vanilla ice cream.

FAB FOR THE FREEZER
This pudding freezes brilliantly. Defrost thoroughly before reheating in the microwave for about 1 minute on high or until piping hot.

EASY CHRISTMAS PUDDING

This pudding is SO easy to make and tastes great. The slow cooker makes easy work of the cooking, as you won't need to continually check to see if it has boiled dry – it won't!

Generously butter a 1.2 litre (2 pint) pudding basin (check that this will fit into your slow cooker dish first) and line the bottom with a small square piece of buttered foil. Chop the figs, prunes and apricots into small 5mm (¼in) pieces (about the same size as the sultanas) and place in a large mixing bowl together with the remaining fruit. Pour over the Marsala or brandy and orange juice, mix well and cover. Leave overnight or until all the liquid is absorbed.

The next day, add the remaining ingredients to the boozy fruit and beat until smooth. Spoon the mixture into the prepared pudding basin. Lightly butter a piece of foil and make a pleat in the centre to allow the pudding to rise. Press this tightly over the pudding basin and push the foil down around the edges. Tie in place with kitchen string, and make a string handle to make lifting the hot basin in and out of the slow cooker easier.

Scrunch up some foil to make a small cushion on which to rest the pudding basin. Place this in the slow cooker dish and top with the pudding. Carefully pour enough boiling water around the outside to come about halfway up the sides of the basin. Cover with the lid and cook on high for 6–10 hours (6 hours will produce a light pudding, and it will become darker and richer as the time passes).

Remove the basin from the slow cooker and place on a heatproof surface. Unwrap the pudding and discard the foil. Run the tip of a knife around the edge to loosen, then, using a tea towel to protect your hands, carefully invert the pudding onto a plate to turn out. Serve warm with brandy sauce (see page 142).

TRY...

to get organised by making this pudding in advance. You can make it up to two months ahead. After cooking, leave the pudding to cool completely, then discard the foil and replace with a new piece. Store in the fridge or freezer until needed (if freezing, defrost thoroughly before reheating). To reheat the pudding on Christmas Day, cook for about 2 hours or until piping hot, then invert over a plate and serve.

Preparation time: 15 minutes, plus soaking
Cooking time: 6–10 hours
Serves 6–8
Vegetarian

100g (3½oz) butter, softened, plus extra for greasing

100g (3½oz) ready-to-eat dried figs

100g (3½oz) ready-to-eat dried prunes

100g (3½oz) ready-to-eat dried apricots

100g (3½oz) ready-to-eat dried cranberries

100g (3½oz) sultanas

4 tbsp Marsala or brandy

Zest and juice of 2 oranges

75g (3oz) white breadcrumbs

75g (3oz) plain flour

2 tsp ground mixed spice

50g (2oz) roughly chopped blanched almonds

200g (7oz) soft light brown sugar

2 large eggs

INDEX

ABOUT THE AUTHOR

Katie Bishop is a successful food writer and stylist. Her love of food led her to enter the acclaimed Young Cook of Britain competition at the age of 14. Katie beat over 32,000 entrants to win, giving her the opportunity to work alongside some of Britain's most renowned chefs.

Katie has worked as a chef around the world but is now based in London. She regularly writes for food magazines, contributes to online sites, pens bestselling cookbooks and appears as a guest chef on TV.

KATIE'S ACKNOWLEDGEMENTS
With thanks to my amazing family – Rupert & Darcey; Mum & Dad; Simon & Sophie. X